LEADER TO LEADER

NUMBER 60 SPRING 2011

HESSELBEIN & COMPANY

EXECUTIVE FORUM

FROM THE FRONT LINES

FROM THE EDITORS

One of the guiding precepts of this journal is that leadership is not about up and down or a position at the top of a pyramid. Leadership is everyone's job. And it's a matter of how to be—not how to do. The articles in this issue amply illustrate and expand on these themes.

Best-selling authors James M. Kouzes and Barry Z. Posner write, "Leadership begins with you. The quest for leadership, therefore, is first an inner quest to discover who you are and what you care about." Drawing on the stories of exemplary leaders, they argue that all effective leaders must make this inner journey. Developing your ability to lead, they show, "is not about stuffing in a whole bunch of new information or trying out the latest technique. It's about leading out of what is already in your soul. It's about liberating the leader within you."

"Leaders usually know the correct way to lead others, so why don't they do it?" Richard L. Daft asks. Too often, Daft says, leaders focus on getting the best out of other people without the necessary preparation, ignoring the truth that "the first job of leadership is often getting the best out of yourself." Personal mastery is essential, yet difficult to achieve. Why do we find it so difficult to lead ourselves, and what steps can we take to achieve this difficult task? Daft offers new and insightful answers to these questions.

Larry and Meagan Johnson tackle the thorny issue of managing up the generational ladder. As Boomers

Leadership is everyone's job.

postpone retirement, many Gen X and Gen Y leaders find themselves in the awkward position of managing people who are older than themselves and have much more experience. The Johnsons—a father-and-daughter team—offer four keys to younger leaders on working well with their older counterparts.

Trust building is a primary imperative for leaders: organizational distrust lowers employee desire to contribute to productivity goals and it breeds fear and a host of destructive behaviors. To address the challenge of distrust, Pamela S. Shockley-Zalabak and Sherwyn P. Morreale present a model for trust building in organizations that is both research based and practice driven; it is designed to produce the staying power that only trust can generate. In this article, they explain the five key drivers of trust: competence, openness and honesty, concern for employees and stakeholders, reliability, and identification.

In the last issue of *Leader to Leader* (No. 59, Winter 2011) Robert Bruce Shaw and Michael M. Chayes discussed the four stages of a successful transition into a new leadership role, with a focus on an initial "discovery" phase. In Part II of their article in this issue, they discuss the questions that each new leader will need to answer in the remaining three transitional stages: *Define:* Mapping out key priorities and strategies; *Deliver:* Sustaining focus and ensuring progress; and *Build:* Building productive relationships with stakeholders.

Vinita Bali, a leader in India who is ranked among the top 50 businesswomen in the world by the *Financial Times,* writes, "Leadership is a capability that each of us has within us. It is formed as we take on the opportunities and challenges of everyday life, and it is measured by our successes and failures." She explains why the most important leadership lessons come from the things we learn every day: "Leadership is less about what we do and more about what we become."

Harvard Business School professor Paul R. Lawrence examines recent advances in brain research and argues that they offer the potential of "a true science of leadership." He explains how our brains have evolved to incorporate four basic drives—to acquire, defend, bond, and comprehend—and that effective decision making draws on each of these drives. Citing a variety of examples, he shows that leaders who take these drives seriously "have a chance, whatever their natural gifts as leaders, to become even better—to replace at least some of the guesswork of leadership with applied knowledge."

In examining successful and unsuccessful leadership, Paul B. Thornton identifies four critical dimensions that make the difference: seeing what is, seeing what is possible, explaining ideas to others, and implementing effective action. And he details the common pitfalls in each of these dimensions that can bring leaders down.

We hope this issue contributes to your own journey in leadership. We welcome your thoughts. Please e-mail us at editor@leadertoleader.org or write to us at

Managing Editor

Leader to Leader

320 Park Avenue, Third Floor

New York, NY 10022

LEADER TO LEADER

Frances Hesselbein
Editor-in-Chief

Alan Shrader
Managing Editor

Peter Economy
Stephen Bernhut
Associate Editors

David Famiano
Editorial Director

Ross Horowitz
Composition / Production Editor

Elizabeth Phillips
Editorial Assistant

Hilary Powers
Copy Editor

Yvo Riezebos
Creative Director

Yvo Riezebos Design
Design

Corbis/Gabriel Beltran
Cover image

Leader to Leader Institute

*"To strengthen the leadership
of the social sector"*

Leader to Leader ISBN 978-1-118-0255-0 is published quarterly by the Leader to Leader Institute and Wiley Subscription Services, Inc., A Wiley Company, at Jossey-Bass, 989 Market St., San Francisco, CA 94103-1741. Copyright © 2011 by the Leader to Leader Institute. All rights reserved. Debra Hunter, President, Jossey-Bass; Susan Lewis, Vice President and Publisher; Peter Sanderson, Director of Marketing; Julianne Ososke, Senior Manufacturing Supervisor; Joe Schuman, Subscriptions Manager; Roger Hunt, Renewals Manager. Permission to copy: No part of this issue may be reproduced in any form without permission in writing from the Leader to Leader Institute and Jossey-Bass. For inquiries, write Permissions Dept., c/o John Wiley & Sons, Inc., 111 River Street, Hoboken, NJ 07030. Periodicals Postage Paid at San Francisco, CA, and additional mailing offices. Postmaster: Send address changes to Leader to Leader, Jossey-Bass, 989 Market St., San Francisco, CA 94103-1741. Indexed by ABI/Inform Database (ProQuest) and Current Abstracts (EBSCO).

Subscriptions: $1,220 institutions. $199 individuals. $99 U.S. 501(c)(3) nonprofit organizations. To order: call toll-free (888) 378-2537, fax toll-free (888) 481-2665, write Jossey-Bass, 989 Market Street, San Francisco, CA 94103-1741, or e-mail jbsubs@jbp.com. Outside the United States, call (415) 433-1767 or fax (415) 951-8553. For article reprints of 100 copies or more, please call Craig Woods at (201) 748-8771 or e-mail cwoods@wiley.com.

BRIGHT FUTURE

by Frances Hesselbein

Occasionally, I casually remark in speeches that I have tattoos on both shoulders. I pause and wait for the audience's shock to become apparent, and then go on to mention that the tattoos are in invisible ink—you can't see them, but I know they are there—several of them.

Always the first tattoo is the reminder, "To serve is to live." Another is Peter Drucker's, "Think first, speak last." Another comes from Drucker's saying, "The leader of the future asks; the leader of the past tells." So my tattoo is, "Ask, don't tell." On the other shoulder is my own distillation from long ago that is ever more significant today: "Leadership is a matter of how to be, not how to do." Below it, "We manage for the mission, we manage for innovation, and we manage for diversity." ("Or we are part of the past" is the unwritten end of the last invisible tattoo.)

Forgive me for sharing something so personal as my invisible tattoos, but today these are my battle cries. They represent a philosophy tested over a long, long journey, and they are as fresh and compelling as the day their messages became part of who I am.

On our website, you can read accounts of the Celebration on November 1 at Michael's restaurant in New York, where 135 guests came together over dinner to celebrate my birthday. (I don't do birthdays, so Liz Edersheim and Ken Witty, the co-conspirators who planned and managed the event, did all of it without my involvement. Even in calling it "the Celebration.") I was told to show up at 6:00 PM at Michael's.

A video tribute to my life and work, "To Serve Is to Live," was shown that even included three members of Girl Scout Troop 17 in Johnstown, Penn. I was their

Girl Scout leader when they were 10 years old and my little boy was even younger. The whole evening became a family affair and guests who had never met became friends. I was overwhelmed then; I am overwhelmed now, and always will be.

I had nothing to do with the guest list, yet everyone there, from General and Mrs. Eric Shinseki, some West Point faculty members, and Tom Moran (chairman, president, and CEO of Mutual of American Life Insurance Company) to the surgeon who saved my life long ago, had been a close and important part of the journey. And friends invited but unable to attend sent messages that touched my heart.

Ken Witty had gone into my personal archives, and there were huge photographs on easels around the room. One was of me at two years old, with blond bangs and a smile. Another showed me at Camp Blue Knob—the Girl Scout Camp on top of the second-highest mountain in Pennsylvania where I was camp director—with the richly diverse camp staff, assembled at a time when diversity was not as valued as it later became. One was of being welcomed by the president of India when I chaired an International Conference sponsored by UNESCO and the World Association of Girl Guides and Girls Scouts in New Delhi, with college student Girl Guides and Girl Scouts from all over the world. Early Girl Scout uniforms, complete with little white gloves, added to this glimpse of the past of some of our early fellow travelers.

Guests loved the photographs of Halston, who designed a new Girl Scout uniform for adults as his contribution to our work, and six years later Bill Blass did the same, and they applauded clips of three presidents of the United States: President Reagan,

"Ask, don't tell."

"Leadership is a matter of how to be, not how to do."

the first President Bush, and President Clinton—all generous friends of the Girl Scouts of the USA and the Drucker Foundation/Leader to Leader Institute, and all fellow travelers along the way.

Tributes were given by Thomas Moran, General Eric Shinseki, Colonel Thomas Kolditz, Robert Buford, Cathy Kloninger, Frank Wicks, Tamara Woodbury, and Tina Doeffer, all moving and generous.

This is a very personal column, for I wanted to share with you a beautiful moment on the journey we share. I still find that evening with friends, family, and all of those present and celebrating an overwhelming, enormously loving, and moving moment always to be remembered. All guests now have a copy of the tribute DVD—"To Serve Is to Live." You can view it on our website.

By the time you read this, the December holidays will be over, with all of us having much to be grateful for. In January, my new book—*My Life in Leadership: The Journey and Lessons Learned Along the Way*—was published. It is my autobiography, and it was difficult to write something so personal, but my publisher, Jossey-Bass, a Wiley imprint, and Alan Shrader, my editor, gave me the courage to be as personal as I needed to be. So it's done, it's out there, it is the story of my life.

April 28 will be the last event in my two-year appointment to the West Point Class of '51 Chair for the Study of Leadership. The list of leaders who have traveled to West Point with me to engage in our Leadership Dialogues and the few yet to come before the end of April is remarkable:

Thomas Moran

LTG Lloyd Austin III

Alan Mulally

Dr. Leonard Schlesinger

Jim Collins

Marshall Goldsmith

Working with cadets and faculty at West Point has been one of the most inspiring privileges of my life.

Now I look forward to 2011 with all of you. Just two words convey my fond wishes for the new decade we will share: *bright future*. It will be bright because all of us together will find ways to make a difference—to serve is to live.

Frances Hesselbein is editor-in-chief of Leader to Leader, founding president of the Drucker Foundation, president and CEO of the Leader to Leader Institute, and former chief executive officer of the Girl Scouts of the U.S.A.

LEADERSHIP LESSONS FROM EVERYDAY LIFE

by Vinita Bali

A lot has been written about people who shape and change companies and other organizations and what makes them who they are and do what they do. Equally, there are larger numbers of people who lead everyday exemplary lives but who go unnoticed. What leadership lessons can we learn from such people? What makes them disciplined and empathetic, with an unwavering focus on the end goal, as they strive for excellence and perfection?

Leadership is a capability that each of us has within us. It is formed as we take on the opportunities and challenges of everyday life, and it is measured by our successes and failures. It is my belief and experience that the leadership lessons we learn in our everyday lives can and should be carried with us into our work environments, and that they can help us become better leaders of our people.

As I have reflected on leadership over the years based on my own experiences across several countries and continents, I have been inspired by people everywhere, irrespective of their country or their socioeconomic status, who exemplify the true qualities of leadership. And they do so by the strength of their character and their authenticity—by the way they live their lives every day. I admire and respect them because their motivation is pure, and they live on the strength of their conviction.

Across all domains and disciplines, leadership is about the human spirit and human endeavor, underpinned by core values that define character. It is this spirit and endeavor that makes the difference in the form and quality of accomplishment. Howard Gardner has talked about leadership as the capacity to continually create. That capacity, infused with the relentless drive for excellence that is inspirational, creates enduring success—whether we talk about successful sports people, successful artists and composers, successful companies, or successful professionals in any field.

In the sections that follow, I explore some of the key lessons from everyday life.

Character and Authenticity Are Core to a Leader

More than anything else, leadership is about character and authenticity. It is about taking ownership for changing something and making it better than you found it. And when that change operates with responsibility, it earns respect. Leadership is exercised every day—in schools, homes, and other institutions. In this article, I look at it from the corporate lens, though its central premise holds everywhere.

The word *character* comes from an ancient Greek verb that means "to engrave," and its related noun meaning "mark" or "distinctive quality." General Schwarzkopf said, "The main ingredient of good leadership is good character. This is because leadership involves conduct and conduct is determined by values." Simply stated, character is about doing the right thing and not letting anything get in the way. Examples of "doing the right thing" abound in the world of business, art, sports, medicine, and many other fields. The common thread of human endeavor and human spirit is what defines leaders. I believe it was Elvis Presley who said that "values are like fingerprints, nobody's are the same, but you leave them all over in everything you do."

At a time when CEO tenures are shrinking to an average of six years across the Fortune 500 companies,

Leadership is a capability within each of us.

"Values are like fingerprints."

management educators and the corporate world must necessarily reflect on the quality of leadership, for that will determine the quality of the world we are all going to live in. Tony Hayward lost his job at BP, not just because of the Gulf of Mexico oil spill (oil spills have happened before) but because of the way he handled the situation and the lack of leadership and ownership he displayed for addressing the problem once it had occurred.

The interesting thing about leadership behavior is that it must be displayed in major moments but is created in the small ones over time. Reputation is based on the integrity and consistency of words and actions—repeatedly.

Leadership Is About Handling Adaptive Challenges

Despite the general convergence of views that technical and functional skills are essential but not enough to succeed in any field, management education continues to place great significance on precisely those aspects—analytical and conceptual abilities, critical thinking, and problem solving—and not enough on adaptive skills. What distinguishes effective leaders from others is not just their technical or functional expertise, but their ability to handle adaptive challenges, that is, those situations or circumstances that cannot be predicted but can occur at any time in the course of business.

Contrast the handling of the 2010 BP Gulf of Mexico oil spill with the dialysis filter crisis that confronted Baxter in Europe in August 2001, when approximately 50 deaths were reported in Spain and Croatia following the use of the company's dialysis filters.

Even though, at first, all investigations were inconclusive as to the cause of death of these patients, the commonality was that these filters came from the same lot and were manufactured by Althin Medical AB, a company that Baxter had acquired in March 2000. Harry Kraemer, the CEO of Baxter, immediately owned up to the situation, apologized for the malfunctioning of these filters, took full responsibility for what happened, asked the Board to reduce his bonus, and put in place standards and processes to prevent a repeat occurrence.

True Leadership Calls for Alignment Between Moral Compass and Behavior

One of the greatest leaders of the twentieth century, Mahatma Gandhi, changed the course of history—not just for India but for many other parts of the world as well—by the courage of his convictions and his authenticity. He epitomized what successful leaders do: he created a sense of purpose and shared vision, he challenged existing ways of thinking, and he energized purposeful action. His moral compass, purpose, and behavior were fully and always aligned.

Gandhi is perhaps the only transformational leader in recent times who held no public office and who has not been given any formal award—either in his lifetime or posthumously. Yet he is one leader who, even six decades after his death, continues to inspire people globally. He did something else that effective leaders do—he listened empathetically to people, even as he fortified his resolve to transform the reality of India. He formulated his ideas of independence, and the broad strategy for getting it, by first traveling extensively around the country to see and hear about the problems and issues faced by ordinary people. He neither delegated nor outsourced that work to anyone else. He was always there, in the midst of his people, inspiring them to action through the sheer brilliance of his strategy and the sense of purpose he instilled in what he said and did.

The story of Gandhi is multifaceted, and a key facet of the story is his indomitable will and character—the endurance to hold to his purpose without vacillation and with thought and action always aligned. In this, he carried with him everyday people, molding and shaping their thinking.

When I worked at the Coca-Cola Company in Atlanta, I had the privilege of meeting Mohammad Ali, who, in response to a question on what makes a champion, said, "Champions aren't made in gyms. Champions are made from something they have deep inside them—a desire, a dream, a vision."

Being Yourself—Every Day

The silent majority of people (the real champions), wake up every morning and bring their best to what they do. They don't necessarily lead companies or countries (in a conventional sense) and they can be found everywhere—from the flower seller to the schoolteacher to the farmer, to moms and dads who believe in character and authenticity and who are driven by a set of values that provide the moral compass for all their actions. We don't write about them often because they occur every day, but if we stop to listen and observe, we can see exemplary behaviors, not in search of recognition but manifesting what is right in the absolute sense and not contextually. It is this vast majority in every organization, in every nation, that can be harnessed to produce extraordinary results, as is empirically evident.

The culture and environment in an organization are influenced not just by top management but by the ability

Leadership must be displayed in major moments but is created in small ones.

of top management to inspire and motivate people to take the right actions. According to Jim Collins, good to great organizations have three forms of discipline: disciplined people, disciplined thought, and disciplined action, thereby eliminating the need for hierarchy, bureaucracy, or controls.

Warren Bennis said, "Becoming a leader is synonymous with becoming yourself. It is precisely that simple and also that difficult." So the question is, how do we get there? Where do awareness and learning and training come from?

From a corporate perspective the demands of leadership are intense and the spotlight seldom leaves you. But the corporate world also creates a set of expectations that at times cause people to behave in ways that may not be truly desirable, either from a governance perspective or from a moral perspective. The failures have less to do with strategy and execution and more to do with the judgment of people in positions of power, where they either make the wrong choices or make convenient choices because the alternatives are hard.

Making Big Ideas Real

In my experience, everyday people can become extraordinary leaders when they have a compelling vision to change the world around them for the better. But they don't just have big ideas, they turn them into reality.

I have selected three stories that embody the human spirit and endeavor I discussed earlier and that underscore the exceptional willingness and courage to change

Extraordinary leaders don't just have big ideas, they turn them into reality.

the rules. In each of the stories there is a profound leadership insight:

- The first story is that of Thimakka, an uneducated and poor casual worker who lives in a village in the south of India. Her story has moved several people and has been shared through prose, poetry, music, and dance. Thimakka is a true environmentalist even though she received no formal education. She and her husband started taking saplings from banyan trees that grew in the village and planting these along a road. From 10 in the first year, Thimakka planted 284 banyan trees along a 4 km stretch of highway. These saplings were planted just before the monsoon so they would get sufficient rainwater to take root and grow.

Thimakka had no resources but she was resourceful and galvanized an entire village through a compelling sense of purpose and accomplishment. She led by example, undaunted by her poverty and not letting anything get in the way of this dream for her village.

- Aravind Eye Care Hospital began with a dream to eliminate unnecessary blindness in India. With its humble beginnings in 1976, in a small town called Madurai in the state of Tamil Nadu in southern India, Aravind Eye Care is changing the world of blindness through an insight that led to the creation of an exceptional business model that is sustainable because it is profitable. The unique insight was that, of the nearly 24 million blind people in the world, about one-third could be treated with a medical intervention. However, in many cases this intervention requires surgery, and there weren't enough surgeons to cope with this requirement! So, Aravind Eye Care concentrated on increasing a surgeon's productivity— and it did so by a factor of ten—by perfecting the technique of assembly line surgery. (The inspiration for this came to one of the founding members as a result of observing how McDonald's ran its operation!) Remarkably, Aravind Eye Care has created a business model where 30 percent of the paying patients enable the remaining 70 percent to be treated free. The business makes a 35 percent operating profit, which in turn is plowed back into expansion.

The dream of an individual changed the lives of many. What began as an 11-bed hospital in the house of the founder (Dr. Venkataswamy, or Dr. V. as he is popularly known) is now a hospital that treats 2.4 million outpatients and performs over 285,000 cataract surgeries every year. Aravind hires paramedical staff from rural and backward areas, trains them, and gives them more responsibility than other institutions do. So it is not the education that is the differentiator—but the attitude, training, and trust that is invested in people.

- Another well-known inspirational leadership story comes from Bangladesh: the Grameen Bank, founded by an individual, Muhammed Yunus, who believed that the way out of poverty was economic freedom and that the poor have skills that are underutilized. Therefore, if credit could be given to the poor, based on potential, through access to microfinance and technology, they would work themselves out of poverty. Grameen Bank has broken all stereotypes by extending micro loans to women and others who have no collateral that have consistently been repaid.

Grameen Bank's success is in a large measure due to its unique structure, which while being formal also incorporates participatory and collaborative approaches, providing effective linkages with existing community structures and the government. These are pivotal to the entire delivery of savings and credit structures. Muhammad Yunus is a leader who has translated and crafted a practical business model that addresses poverty in a fundamental way, by developing and providing an important instrument called micro-finance.

It Is Not What We Do But What We Become

The common thread across all these stories is that they revolve around everyday individuals who did not oc-

cupy any formal office, and yet who significantly affected the thoughts, feelings, and behavior of a large number of other people, to create something truly meaningful and profound. These leaders have not just fashioned stories but embodied these stories into their everyday life. In that sense they have demonstrated that leadership is less about what we do and more about what we become—and in the process—how we influence and learn from those around us.

Vinita Bali is the CEO and managing director of Britannia Industries Limited, a leading food company in India. Prior to this she held marketing and general management roles in preeminent multinationals like the Coca-Cola Company and Cadbury Schweppes PLC and has lived and worked in six countries and five continents. She has won several awards and accolades for her marketing acumen and business leadership: She was named "Businesswoman of the Year—2009" by the Economic Times and was ranked 21st among the world's top 50 businesswomen by the Financial Times.

WHAT LEADERS NEED TO KNOW ABOUT HUMAN EVOLUTION AND DECISION MAKING

by Paul R. Lawrence

Engineering advanced enormously once it gained a foundation in physics. For medicine, the advance was even more profound once it gained a foundation in biology and chemistry. But leadership, although essential to all societies, has never taken the equivalent step from art to science. As a result, we still see leadership ranging in effectiveness from brilliant to inept and in morality from inspirational to demonic.

I believe, however, that recent research into the workings of the human brain as it makes decisions, combined with recent research into the turning points in our own evolution, now offers the building blocks for a true science of leadership. In this article, I consider the biological underpinnings of leadership and their impact on organizations.

From Instinct to Decision Making

The evolution of early humans resulted in a brain that is unique in many ways. One of the most important is the way it decides what to do in a given set of circumstances. Other animals typically survive because they have evolved specialized physical traits and behavioral instincts suited to a particular environment. Humans are different. We do have some instincts, but they account for a very small portion of what we do. Instead, early humans became able to take a wide variety of information (including memory) into account and figure out what to do. And while early humans were not individually very strong, quick, or deadly, they became very effective in groups. An important reason for this is that they could take risks because they could trust their companions to help them rather than opportunistically rob or abandon them. This sort of cooperation was a radical innovation and gave early humans an enormous advantage over much more powerful creatures.

Such improvisatory and cooperative behavior, in contrast to the instinctive behavior of other animals, relied on a brain that could make unique circumstance-driven decisions rather than summon up instincts. In particular, these decisions had to take into account the benefit of one's fellows as well as one's own survival—even when these two imperatives seemed to be in conflict with each other. The capacity for this kind of decision making is the foundation of complex human societies, of organizations of all kinds, and of leadership.

The Four Drives

How does all this apply to the everyday practice of leadership? Let's look at how this unique decision-making process works inside the brain. Humans evolved four basic drives, each operating independently in the brain, each essential for our survival as a species, and each an equal component of good leadership:

- The drive to acquire—to get what we need or value—from food, shelter, and offspring to promotion, expertise, or excitement.

- The drive to defend—to protect what we need or value, including our company's market share and reputation.

- The drive to bond—to form long-term, trusting, caring relationships that may provide *but are not limited to* mutual benefit. These include relationships with coworkers, customers, suppliers, and investors.

Research now offers the building blocks for a true science of leadership.

- The drive to comprehend—to make sense of the world and ourselves, which includes forecasting, inventing, and problem solving.

Each of these drives is constantly receiving information from our sense organs and each responds with its own imperative. Imagine a CEO whose company has just lost a key long-term contract because a competitor's prices have recently dropped. The drive to acquire makes it look desirable to push the sales team harder. The drive to comprehend inspires efforts to find out how the competitor was able to lower its prices. The drive to defend suggests cutting staff while trying to recover lost business. The drive to bond says not to cast loyal and experienced employees overboard, especially in such a high-unemployment economy. As we see, the last two imperatives are in direct conflict.

I emphasize here that these four drives are not a metaphor; they are actual brain functions. Using a variety of research tools and techniques, ranging from MRI scans to field studies, researchers can see different parts of this decision-making process in action. For example, brain-imaging studies have shown one part of the brain (the nucleus acumbens in the limbic area) "lighting up" with increased blood flow when people who had been asked to think about either making a donation to a charity or keeping the money for themselves chose to think about donating—the drive to bond in action.

The Four-Drive Decision

Amazingly, the variety and even conflict of the drives is not the problem—it is the solution. It sets in motion a process in which a different part of our

> *The drives conflict is not the problem—it is the solution.*

CEO's brain, the prefrontal cortex, when it receives the various imperatives from the four drives, pulls in relevant knowledge and experience stored in other parts of the brain and formulates possible courses of action that are reviewed to see how the drives will respond. This decision-making process continues until it arrives at a solution that is at least "good enough" for all four drives.

What we can see here are all the elements of good leadership. Good leaders are concerned with the organization's (or team's) survival and success. But they ensure survival and success by taking as much as possible into account—not only as much information as possible, but also as many of the stakeholders as possible. We admire a business leader such as Steve Jobs because he consistently seems to take not only his company but his customers—and not only his present customers but millions of potential customers—into account. Apple is characterized by a powerful drive to bond as well as obvious drives to acquire, defend, and comprehend. Contrast that with the Wall Street financial leaders who managed—for a while—to amass great wealth for themselves while doing harm to millions of others touched by their actions.

Four-Drive Leadership in Practice

The decision-making process I have described is not perfect. Honest leaders can blunder. Dishonest leaders—especially when leaders of nations or very large corporations—can do tremendous harm. I believe, however, that a scientifically grounded theory of leadership can help. Knowing that good leadership is a reflection of how our brains are designed to make decisions should make it easier for us to detect when the process isn't working as it should, such as when one drive is overwhelming the others. For business leaders, this is an acute problem because their circumstances seem—and I emphasize the word *seem*—to demand that the drive to acquire should dominate almost all decisions.

Because we have evolved to survive by taking all four drives into account, it should not be too surprising that companies can actually improve their performance when they do take all four drives into account. An oil company, for example, improved the social culture, the safety record, and the business performance of two offshore rigs by attending to all four drives rather than just the drives to acquire and defend. (These are the two drives that any animal has, and it is no coincidence that a supervisor on one of the oil rigs recalled some of his men acting like "a pack of lions.") Although no one involved had ever heard of my four-drive theory of leadership, the workers' comments show an awareness that their drives to bond and to comprehend, long suppressed, were finally being addressed. The results were beneficial to them, to their families, and to the company's bottom line—and therefore to its investors.

How Four-Drive Leadership Applies to Groups

To be effective, leaders must take into account how the four drives affect the following group characteristics:

- Purpose
- Competencies
- Trust building
- Motivation

Group Purpose

Good leadership provides a clear collective purpose that is linked to fulfilling the four drives of the group's various stakeholders. Of course, these can conflict and the leader has to balance them just as the prefrontal cortex balances conflicting drives in the individual brain. For example, the motto "the customer is always right" can be recast as, "Sales staff should give any customer with a reasonable request as much help and as much information as possible rather than keeping that assistance within predetermined limits." That is, the customer should be gratified (drive to acquire), protected (drive to defend), befriended (drive to bond), and informed (drive to comprehend) to the extent possible. At the same time, the employee—and the company—tries to gain a satisfied customer (drive to acquire and to bond), avoid bad word-of-mouth (drive to defend), and learn something about what is making customers happy or unhappy (drive to comprehend). Many managers would fear leaving such apparently complex decisions in the hands of their staff, but in fact, this is just the sort of decision our brains are designed to make. (That doesn't mean that inexperienced staff don't need to be trained first.)

Group Competencies

An effective group is made up of people with different skills, such as accounting or salesmanship, different personality traits, such as decisiveness or friendliness, and different resources, such as physical endurance or well-placed connections. It is a leader's job to consider the four drives of all these various people—and to consider that *all* of them have all four drives. For example, salespeople obviously need to know what the company's marketing strategy is, but, in fact, all

Companies can improve their performance when they take all four drives into account.

Humans evolved to trust each other, given the chance.

employees have a drive to comprehend and would like to know more about the larger effort of which they are a part. You'll be surprised by what use they can make of such information if you provide it. In one company, the maintenance team made important cost-cutting suggestions because they saw every day what was being thrown out. If no one had brought them in on the company's cost-cutting drive, they would have just kept "doing their job" and throwing out the trash.

Group Trust Building

Trust lubricates group relationships and can be a major competitive advantage. Distrust, on the other hand, is expensive, making all manner of internal and external exchanges slower, more complicated, and more fragmented. Humans have evolved to trust each other, given the chance—that is how we survived without the physical strength and specialized instincts of other hunting species. The crews on the oil rigs were able to be more productive once they didn't have to channel so much energy into bullying each other just to feel safe from each other.

Group Motivation

It has been estimated that organizations suffer up to $370 billion in lost productivity every year in the United States alone due to workers "not feeling engaged." It is no accident that a 2008 study found that about 60 percent of the variation in employee motivation can be accounted for by how well the organization fulfills all four drives of its employees.

Taking Leadership from Art to Science

A scientific theory of leadership shows that the normal human brain is the leadership brain. We have evolved to survive by meeting our own needs and the needs of others *as part of the same decision-making process within the brain.* Leaders who take these findings seriously have a chance, whatever their natural gifts as leaders, to become even better—to replace at least some of the guesswork of leadership with applied knowledge.

Paul R. Lawrence is the Wallace Brett Donham Professor of Organizational Behavior Emeritus at Harvard Business School and the author of "Driven to Lead: Good, Bad, and Misguided Leadership." During his 44 years on the Harvard faculty, he taught in all the school's programs and served as chairman of the Organizational Behavior unit and of both the MBA program and the Advanced Management Program for senior executives. Lawrence has published 25 books and numerous articles focusing on the human aspects of management.

WHY SOME LEADERS SUCCEED AND OTHERS FAIL

by Paul B. Thornton

As a high school hockey player, I always wondered why some teams overachieved and others floundered. And I discovered that sometimes weaker teams showed dramatic improvement when a new coach took charge. That sparked my interest in leadership. Later, at Ohio University, I took Dr. Paul Hersey's course, "Managing Organizational Behavior." His class further ignited my interest in leadership.

In studying, interviewing, and working with many leaders over the past 20 years, I've found the best leaders excel at four things:

- Seeing what is—current reality

- Identifying opportunities—determining what's possible

- Explaining their ideas—convincing others to take action

- Implementing change

Seeing What Is—Current Reality

Leaders see the big picture and at times bore down into the details. I call it the "T" approach. The horizontal part of the "T" refers to getting a broad understanding of the current situation; for example, what are the big challenges facing the organization? The vertical part of the "T" refers to probing into the details.

In his book *Good to Great: Why Some Companies Make the Leap . . . and Others Don't*, author Jim Collins says that great leaders have the discipline to confront the most brutal facts about the current situation. They cut through the hype and spin to uncover the truth. They ask tough questions, face challenges squarely, and analyze both hard and soft data.

- The challenges: What are the challenges the people and organization are facing? For example, the organization may be dealing with the loss of a major customer, new competition, government regulators, or high turnover.

- The hard data: Hard data refers to the numbers. The numbers tell a story about what's happening with sales, expenses, and profit, as well as anything else being measured. It's useful to look at today's numbers as well as the trends.

- The soft data: Soft data refers to hard-to-measure things such as people's hopes, dreams, fears, and frustrations.

In assessing the current situation, it is important to get feedback from multiple points of view, including customers, employees, managers, stockholders, suppliers, and external consultants. Once collected, the data must be organized, interpreted, and analyzed. All the pieces of the puzzle must be put together to have a coherent picture of today's reality.

Not Seeing Current Reality

In *Why Smart Executives Fail*, Sydney Finkelstein examines more than 50 of the world's most notorious business failures. His analysis indicates that in most instances, the executives failed to see or accept

All the pieces of the puzzle must be put together.

what was actually happening. In some cases, they were blinded by their own prior successes. In other cases, they inexplicably held tenaciously to a vision despite clear evidence that the chosen strategic direction was ill-advised.

Here are some of the problems that limit a leader's ability to see reality clearly:

- *Blind Spots:* Leaders who have big egos are blind to ideas that don't align with their own.

- *Yes People:* These individuals tell leaders only what they want to hear.

- *Fear:* Some leaders are afraid to face the most sensitive and difficult problems.

- *Bias:* Deep-seated stereotypes and biases cause some leaders to inaccurately filter what they see and hear.

- *Limited Observations:* A small sample size may cause some leaders to jump to inaccurate conclusions.

What should you as a leader do? Remind yourself to stay open and curious. Ask questions and listen for what's new, not what you already know. Spend time with outliers—those mavericks who see things others often miss.

Bottom line—you need an accurate picture of the current situation. Current reality is the starting point or baseline from which you work.

Identifying Opportunities— Determining What's Possible

Current reality is one thing; what is possible is something quite different. Leaders see opportunities while nonleaders only see the status quo. Sometimes the "opportunity" involves closing the gap between people's words and actions. These are some of the common gaps:

- *Values:* Behavior doesn't align with stated values.

- *Direction:* Current actions don't support the strategy.

- *Performance:* Accomplishments are below potential.

- *Motivation:* Effort is below what is required.
- *Commitment:* People say they are committed but things aren't getting done.

These gaps represent opportunities for leaders to do the following:

1. Raise people's awareness so they see the gap.
2. Rally people to take action to close the gap.

In other situations, leaders connect the dots in new ways. Leaders have the expertise to scan for new ideas and the cognitive ability to see new relationships. Benchmarking, brainstorming, and other creative techniques can help identify new possibilities. "I'm always looking for opportunities, both domestically and foreign," says Summer Redstone, chairman of Viacom. "Opportunity does not knock. You have to find it. Nothing is impossible. Nothing."

Not Discovering Opportunities

Some leaders aren't motivated to search for new opportunities for the following reasons:

- They are fully vested in the current strategy and don't want to change.
- They want to keep doing what made them successful.
- They dread failing—they don't want to identify bold new initiatives because deep down they're afraid they will not succeed.

What should leaders do? First, realize that what was good or great last year may be just average this year. Recognize that there is always something better waiting to be discovered. Benchmark and observe the best performers in all fields. Get out of your comfort zones.

"Opportunity does not knock. You have to find it."

Effective leaders keep it simple.

Force yourself to do something new every day. Explore new ways of thinking about what's possible.

Once you have identified numerous opportunities, the next step is identifying the one to three big ideas that make the most sense. You must prioritize, because you'll never have the energy and resources needed to pursue all the opportunities you identify.

Explaining Your Ideas—Convincing Others to Take Action

Having ideas, proposals, and a vision is one thing. Being able to describe everything in a way that is clear, inspiring, and compelling is something else. The big challenge for organizational leaders is to create a message that is so clear and compelling that all employees, from the machine operator to the C-level executive, understand and see the value in the idea or vision.

Effective leaders keep it simple. In their book *Made to Stick*, authors Chip Heath and Dan Heath suggest that to be simple you need to find the core of the idea. Strip the idea down to its most critical essence. Michael S. Hyatt, CEO of Thomas Nelson Publishers, states, "Leaders remove the clutter so their big ideas stand out." The best communicators use simple examples, stories, and illustrations to explain their ideas.

Leaders not only need to explain their ideas clearly, they must also convince others to take action. Inspirational leaders create a sense of urgency. They explain why it's important to take action now rather than later. In addition, they describe one to three action-

Leaders aren't happy with the status quo.

able steps they want people to take. They motivate people by offering incentives and explaining what's in it for them. Oftentimes they also explain the consequences of not changing.

Leaders are fully committed to their ideas. They deliver their messages with passion and conviction. They have no doubts, hesitation, or questions about the correctness of their ideas and vision.

Not Explaining Your Vision or Convincing Others to Follow

Some leaders miss the mark when presenting their leadership message for the following reasons:

- Providing too much detail. Big ideas are buried in the presentation.

- Not identifying actionable steps for people to take.

- Being unclear as to what's in it for their audience.

- Not conveying passion and enthusiasm in their delivery.

What should a leader do? Simplify! Simplify! Simplify! Get the facts and data that will help you make the business case for change. Explain why you care and why others should care as well. Look at things from the audience's point of view. Be able to explain how your idea(s) will help them. Specify the steps you want them to take. Ask for the sale. Ask for their commitment.

Implementing Change

Some leaders are effective at describing their ideas and vision, yet fail when it comes to actually implementing change. Implementing change requires a strong combination of *both* management and leadership skills.

On the management side, leaders need to plan, organize, measure, control, and motivate employees away from talking and into taking action. In many change initiatives, the leader selects and empowers a competent project manager to handle the management tasks. But in all cases, the leader needs to make sure a detailed plan is established.

On the leadership side, leaders need to inspire people to overcome their fears and frustrations. Leaders must also set the example and be the first to model the changes being implemented.

Effective leaders are flexible and make adjustments and course corrections as needed. In addition, they demonstrate great determination and perseverance to see the vision become a reality. However, not all change initiatives turn out exactly as planned.

Why Leaders Fail When Implementing Change

These are some of the common problems:

- Lack of clarity in terms of conveying who must change and in what ways

- Inadequate training or follow-on support

- Not recognizing or rewarding efforts and early successes

- Choosing an ineffective project manager

What should leaders do? First, be clear on who must change and in what specific ways. Assemble the right team (project manager and implementation team) to get the job done. Train, educate, and keep people informed. Celebrate success early and often.

Beyond the Status Quo

Leaders aren't happy with the status quo. They believe most people and organizations are underperforming. The best leaders explain their ideas for improvement in a clear, concise, and compelling way. They energize people to act in order to achieve a better future. Leaders not only see what's possible but pursue it with passion and determination.

Paul B. Thornton is the author of numerous articles and 13 books on management and leadership. His recent book, "Leadership: Best Advice I Ever Got," highlights the guiding principles of some well-known CEOs. He was a human resources manager and consultant at the Hamilton Standard Division of United Technologies Corporation for 19 years. Thornton has conducted training programs for many companies including UMASS Medical School, Palmer Foundry, Mercy Health Systems, Kuwait Oil Corporation, and United Technologies Corporation. For more information, visit www.PBThornton.com.

LEADERSHIP BEGINS WITH AN INNER JOURNEY

James M. Kouzes and Barry Z. Posner

Everything you will ever do as a leader is based on one audacious assumption. It's the assumption that you matter. Before you can lead others you have to lead yourself and believe that you can have a positive impact on others. You have to believe that your words can inspire and your actions can move others. You have to believe that what you do counts for something. If you don't, you won't even try. Leadership begins with you.

The quest for leadership, therefore, is first an inner quest to discover who you are and what you care about, and it's through this process of self-examination that you find the awareness needed to lead. Self-confidence is really awareness of and faith in your own powers, and these powers become clear and strong only as you work to identify and develop them. The mastery of the art of leadership comes with the mastery of the self, and so developing leadership is a process of developing the self.

Melissa Poe, a fourth grader in Nashville, Tennessee, became very concerned about the natural environment and the kind of world she and her friends might live in if people didn't start paying attention to their everyday actions. After seeing a television program about pollution that portrayed a very scary future, Melissa asked the question, "Will the future be a safe place to live in when I get older?" She decided she had to do something about it. That night she wrote a letter to the president, but Melissa knew the pollution problem wouldn't wait. At home she and her family started recycling, turning lights and faucets off when they weren't in use, and planting trees. Melissa wrote more letters to newspapers, television stations, and more politicians. Melissa also started a club, called Kids F.A.C.E. (Kids For a Clean Environment) so that her friends, who'd been asking how they could help, could do projects together like writing letters, planting trees, and picking up litter. "We knew we were doing small things, but we also knew it took a bunch of small things to make a big difference," she told us.

When after several weeks she still hadn't heard back from the president, Melissa, realizing he was a busy man, felt she needed to do more to get him to see her letter. She decided to make her letter bigger so he couldn't miss it. She called up a billboard company in her home town and asked if they would put up a billboard with her letter to the president. The company donated that billboard and also connected her with other billboard companies, and in a matter of six months, over 250 billboards were put up all over the United States, at least one in each state and one just a mile from the White House.

Almost immediately, Melissa began receiving letters from other kids who were as concerned as she was about the environment. They wanted to help. Just six months after she began her journey to get people's attention about the environment, Melissa appeared on the *Today Show* to tell her story. It is here that Kids F.A.C.E. grew from a local club to a national organization. Starting with just six members at her elementary school, Kids F.A.C.E. grew to more than 2,000 club chapters in 22 countries and more than 350,000 members before Melissa, at age 17, handed over the reins to two 15-year-olds, saying she was too old for the job. (Today there are 500,000 members.)

Is Melissa a leader? Can someone at age 9 or 15 demonstrate the practices of exemplary leadership? Aren't those mainly abilities reserved for people in senior positions in big-time organizations?

Yes, yes, and no. Yes, Melissa is a leader. Yes, you can demonstrate leadership at any age. No, leadership is not about some position in an organization and clearly not just for those in senior positions.

You have to believe that what you do counts for something.

You can demonstrate leadership at any age.

A Process of Internal Self-Discovery

Fast-forward to a recent leadership seminar at the Hong Kong University of Science and Technology and Olivia Lai, who told us that she was initially a little taken aback when we asked her to write about her personal best leadership experience: "Here I am, at 25 years of age, with four years of work experience. How could I possibly have a personal best in leadership?" After further reflection, she realized that in actuality,

It wasn't all that hard to figure out what my personal best was and write about it. Even more surprising is that it became clear that leadership is everywhere, it takes place every day, and leadership can come from anyone. It doesn't matter that you don't have the title of "manager," "director," "CEO," to go with it. In the end, that's all they are . . . titles on business cards and company directories. Being a true leader transcends all that.

Becoming a leader is a process of internal self-discovery. In order for me to become a leader and become an even better leader, it's important that I first define my values and principles. If I don't know what my own values are and determine expectations for myself, how can I set expectations for others? How will I convey confidence, strong will, and empathy? Without looking within myself, it's not possible for me to look at others and recognize their potential and help others become leaders.

"I know who I was, who I am, and where I want to be."

Through her own process of self-discovery, Olivia, like leaders everywhere, realized that becoming a leader begins when you come to understand who you are, what you care about, and why you do what you do. Developing yourself as a leader begins with knowing your own key convictions; it begins with your value system. Clarifying your own values and aspirations is a highly personal matter, and no one else can do it for you. To exhibit harmonious leadership—leadership in which your words and deeds are consonant—you must be in tune internally.

All leaders must take this inner journey. "I know who I was, who I am, and where I want to be," says Dan Kaplan, founder of Daniel Kaplan Associates and former president of Hertz Equipment Rental Corporation. "So in other words," he continues, "I know the level of commitment that I am prepared to make, and why I am personally prepared to make that level of commitment." In this vein values drive the commitment necessary to create leaders in the first place.

Dan's words reflect what leadership scholar Warren Bennis reported in his study of how successful people learned to become leaders: "To become a leader, then, you must become yourself; become the maker of your own life." Warren observes that knowing yourself is "the most difficult task any of us faces. But until you truly know yourself, strengths and weaknesses, know what you want to do and why you want to do it, you cannot succeed in any but the most superficial sense of the word."

Your ultimate success in business and in life depends on how well you know yourself, what you value, and why you value it. The better you know who you are and what you believe in, the better you are at making sense of the often incomprehensible and conflicting demands you receive daily. Do this, or do that. Buy this, buy that. Decide this, decide that. Support this, support that. You need internal guidance to navigate the turbulent waters in this stormy world. A clear set of personal values and beliefs is the critical controller in that guidance system.

You Have to Stand for Something

People won't follow you, or even pay you much attention, if you don't have strong values. In our studies, we've asked thousands of people around the world to list the historical leaders they most admire—leaders, who if they were alive today, they could imagine themselves following willingly. Here are just a few of the names: Susan B. Anthony, Mustafa Kemal Ataturk, Jesus Christ, Mahatma Gandhi, Martin Luther King Jr., Abraham Lincoln, Nelson Mandela, Golda Meir, Mohammed, Eleanor Roosevelt, Franklin D. Roosevelt, Helen Suzman, Mother Teresa, and Margaret Thatcher. The entire list is populated by people with strong beliefs about matters of principle. All were passionate about what was right and just. The message is clear. People are admired because of their unwavering commitment to principles. They stand for something.

People rightfully expect their leaders to have the courage of their convictions. They expect them to stand up for their beliefs. When leaders are clear about what they believe in, they can take strong stands and are much less likely to be swayed by every fad or opinion poll. We've all heard the expression "Leaders stand up for their beliefs." To provide a solid platform on which to stand, your beliefs must be clear to you and clearly communicated to others. When these values are matched by your deeds, then you've earned the credibility required for others to put their trust in you, to willingly climb up and join you on that platform, knowing they'll be supported.

When you're not clear about your personal values it's hard to imagine how you can stand up for your beliefs, isn't it? How can you speak out if you don't know what's important to you? How can you have the courage of your convictions if you have no convictions? Leaders who aren't clear about what they believe are likely to change their position with every shift in public opinion. Without core beliefs and with only shifting positions, would-be leaders are judged as inconsistent and derided for being "political" in their behavior.

After all, who's the very first person you have to lead? Who's the first person who must be willing to follow you? You are, of course. Until you passionately believe in something it's hard to imagine that you could ever convince anyone else to believe. And if you wouldn't follow you, why should anyone else?

Who Are You?

We've asked thousands of people over the years to imagine a scenario where someone walks into the room and announces to them and their colleagues, "Hi, I'm your new leader!" At that very moment, what do you want to know from this person? What are the questions that immediately pop into your mind? While there are lots of questions someone would want to ask that individual, by far the most frequently asked is: "Who are you?"

People want to know your values and beliefs, what you really care about, and what keeps you awake at night. They want to know who most influenced you, the events that shaped your attitudes, and the experiences that prepare you for the job. They want to know what drives you, what makes you happy, and what ticks you off. They want to know what you're like as a person, and why you want to be their leader. They want to know if you play an instrument, compete in sports, go to the movies, or enjoy the theater. They want to know about your family, what you've done, and where you've traveled. They want to un-

derstand your personal story. They want to know why they ought to be following you.

So if you are the new leader who walks into that room one day, you'd better be prepared to answer the "Who are you?" question. And, to answer that question for others, you first have to answer it for yourself. In one of our leadership workshops, our colleague Spencer Clark explained himself to participants in the following way:

> I am the chief learning officer for Cadence Design Systems. I was a division president for Black and Decker, and a manager for General Electric. But these [job titles] are not who I am. If you want to know who I am, you need to understand that I grew up in Kentucky. That I was one of four sons, and we lived on a sharecropper's farm and slept in a home that had no inside plumbing. Who I am is not simply what I do. Knowing who I am has been enormously helpful in guiding me in making decisions about what I would do and how I would do it.

As Spencer makes clear, his job résumé says very little about who he is and why he makes the decisions and takes the actions he does. He knows that there is far more to him than his work history, the titles he's had, and the positions he's held. For Spencer to become the leader that he is, he had to dig beneath the surface and find out more about the events that shaped him, the beliefs that informed him, and the values that guided him. He also knows that it's helpful for others to un-

How can you have the courage of your convictions if you have no convictions?

The clearer you are, the easier it is to stay on the path you've chosen.

derstand those same things before they can commit to his leadership decisions and actions.

During the last few years we've had the opportunity to co-facilitate leadership development programs with Ron Sugar, then chairman and CEO of Northrop Grumman Corporation. At the formal start of every one of these sessions, before he ever uttered a word, Ron would walk to the front of the room, sit down at a piano, and play for a few minutes.

After he'd played his last note, Ron would turn to his senior executive colleagues and ask, "Does anyone know why I began this session with playing the piano?" The point, he'd go on to explain, was that if people are going to follow you they needed to know more about you than the fact that you're their boss. They needed to know something about who you are as a person—your hopes, dreams, talents, expectations, and loves. "Leadership is personal," Ron would proclaim. "Do the people who work for and with you know if you can play the piano?" Ron would ask his colleagues. "Do they know who you are, what you care about, and why they ought to be following you?"

We were sharing this story one day with a group of people from a number of different organizations, and one participant said he could underscore just how important this point was by telling his own story about their new CEO. It seems this new chief executive was making the rounds throughout the company, talking about his vision for the firm and how people needed to execute on it:

The CEO was there supposedly so people could get to know him. So imagine how flabbergasted everyone was when someone asked him, "What do you like to do when you are not working?" and he replied rather curtly, "That's a personal matter and not relevant; next question."

But, that's the point, isn't it! Who is this guy? What does he really care about? Why should we follow—believe and trust—him if we don't know who he is? And he won't tell us!

We could all sense his exasperation. We're all just more reluctant to follow someone if they're unwilling to tell us about themselves. We start to become a little suspicious. We're less willing to trust.

When to Say Yes and When to Say No

If you are ever to become a leader others will willingly follow, you must be transparent to others and known as someone who stands by your principles. And as every would-be leader has discovered, first you have to listen to your inner self in order to discover who you really are and what you are all about. There is no shortage of different interests out there competing for your time, your attention, and your approval. Before you listen to those voices, you have to listen to that voice inside that tells you what's truly important. Only then will you know when to say yes and when to say no—and mean it.

Developing leadership capacity is not about stuffing in a whole bunch of new information or trying out the latest technique. It's about leading out of what is already in your soul. It's about liberating the leader within you. It's about setting yourself free. It's about putting your ear to your heart and just listening. Clarity of values is essential in knowing which way, for each of us, is north, south, east, or west. The clearer you are, the easier it is to stay on the path you've chosen. In exploring your inner territory and finding your voice you calibrate an inner compass by which to navigate the course of your daily life and to take the first steps along the journey of making a difference.

Just as sunlight burns away the morning fog, the more light you shine on what you stand for, what you believe in, and what you care about, the more clearly you'll see those road signs pointing in the direction you want to go. Starting with the inner journey gives you the confidence to take the right turns, to make the tough decisions, to act with determination, and to take charge of your life.

James M. Kouzes is the Dean's Executive Professor of Leadership at the Leavey School of Business Administration, Santa Clara University. He is the 2010 recipient of the Thought Leadership Award from the Instructional Systems Association and was named one of HR Magazine's 2010 Most Influential International Thinkers.

Barry Z. Posner is professor of leadership at Santa Clara University, where he served as dean of the Leavey School of Business for twelve years. He is the recipient of the 2011 Outstanding Scholar Award from the Journal of Management Inquiry.

Together, Jim and Barry are the best-selling authors of "The Leadership Challenge," "A Leader's Legacy," "Credibility," "Encouraging the Heart," "The Leadership Challenge Workbook," and more than a dozen other books and workbooks on leadership. The ideas in this article are included in their newest book, "The Truth About Leadership: The No-Fads, Heart-of-the-Matter Facts You Need to Know," among other "truths." These concepts are further developed in their books "A Leader's Legacy" and "Credibility: How Leaders Gain and Lose It, Why People Demand It."

FIRST, LEAD YOURSELF

Richard L. Daft

Leaders usually know the correct way to lead others, so why don't they do it? When Martha was promoted to sales manager for an advertising agency, she inherited a difficult employee who was a strong producer but whose overbearing competitiveness caused resentment among team members. Martha gathered her facts and scheduled a meeting with the prima donna. As she broached the subject of his behavior, his reaction was defensive, and she backed down. "My overwhelming sense of empathy overrode my ability to be assertive and provide strong direction." She was clearly disappointed in herself. Martha's tendency toward people pleasing overrode her ability to be assertive and do what her department—and her employee—needed. She later reflected, "It was like getting in my car to go east and the car insisted on going west, and I couldn't do anything about it."

Or consider Bob, head of a corporate manufacturing division, who promised himself and others that he would delegate more decisions. Although he was used to making all the hiring decisions himself, Bob asked the sales director to meet with candidates and make the hiring decision for a customer service position. Three weeks later, the director brought his top choice to Bob's office, along with an offer letter for Bob to sign. Dumbfounded, Bob muttered that he wanted to meet the final three candidates himself. He couldn't accept the director's choice, someone with whom he felt

little rapport, so he interviewed the other candidates and hired the person at the bottom of the director's list. "My mind has a mind of its own," he said. It was no surprise when both the sales director and new hire quit within a few months.

Leadership is often described as getting the best out of other people. But as Martha and Bob discovered, the first job of leadership is often getting the best out of yourself. For example, *Fortune* magazine reported a study of 38 failed CEOs. All were good at the cognitive tasks—vision, strategy, ideas—but things broke down at execution. The CEOs' actions did not follow their stated intentions. When leaders know the smarter behavior, why do they get sidetracked into unwanted behavior? Personal mastery is a difficult thing. Most leaders today receive reasonably good feedback about how their leadership could be better. Leaders and managers typically know what they *should* be doing, *how* to do it, and *why* they should do it. Yet often their intentions and behaviors fail to align.

In my consulting and executive teaching, I have come across dozens and dozens of internal conflicts between knowing and executing. One part of a leader wants to do one thing; another part wants to do something else. The theory of constraints is very clear that the weakest link in any system will limit performance, and correcting the weak link will have a big payback in improved performance. Typical leadership weak links are reflected in the following behaviors:

- Micromanaging direct reports
- Procrastinating
- Not following through on commitments
- Making tactless remarks
- Insisting on always being right
- Overreacting and expressing inappropriate anger
- Finding fault with others and being outwardly critical
- Not celebrating and appreciating others' accomplishments
- Not listening
- Talking too much
- Not staying focused
- Showing impatience, such as interrupting others

When leaders have one of these counterproductive behaviors, they often have great difficulty achieving mastery over it. And the negative impact can be huge, because their behavior affects dozens or perhaps hundreds of other people. What is going on that leaders seem unable to alter their behavior to follow their better intentions?

The CEO and the Elephant

According to psychologists and neuroscientists there are two parts to the human brain, and the parts are sometimes in conflict. There is a habitual, automatic, and largely unconscious part of the brain that represents an older system. I call this "the inner elephant" because of the strength of its reactions, unconscious impulses, fears, emotional drives, and lifelong habits. The elephant is strong because its behavior is wired into your nervous system after a lifetime of conditioning. The newer system in the brain represents an intentional, reasoning, thoughtful, and largely conscious mind. This is the brain's executive function, which I am calling "the inner CEO" because it can see the ob-

"It was like getting in my car to go east and the car insisted on going west."

jective big picture and take a balanced approach to determining the best action. The intentional CEO plays a smaller role than the unconscious habitual mind, but its higher-order choice processes can be developed to guide the inner elephant.

The older elephant part of the brain represents a marvelous internal system that has evolved to guide people safely through each day, usually without mishap. It handles memory, language, perception, communication, and other vital information processing. Probably 98 percent of the time our intention and behavior are in alignment. The problem arises when this automatic system is not in alignment with our intentions or with what others want from us, as Martha and Bob discovered. The elephant's circuitry is compelling. If the elephant wants to turn left or right in search of food, it will do so, regardless of a person's conscious wish to be on a diet. Even the apostle Paul said, "I do not understand my own actions. For I do not do what I want, but I do the very thing I hate. I can will what is right, but I cannot do it" (Romans 7:15). Fortunately, even though the elephant's conditioned bad habit is wired in, potential corrective action is available from the CEO part of the brain.

Recognize Your Two Parts

Behavior starts with a thought, and there are clear differences in thoughts originating from the elephant and the CEO parts of the brain. Examples of some traits that the elephant may display compared to the inner CEO are in Table 1. You can learn to recognize when the elephant's dysfunctional pattern is dominant, and when your executive is in charge. Do you recognize any elements of your own behavior in Table 1?

The elephant part of the brain is always on. In Eastern spirituality the flow of random thoughts is called "monkey mind" because it resembles a restless monkey jumping from branch to branch. A restless or racing mind is a clear signal that your elephant is feeling fear or anxiety, and you won't be able to concentrate or think straight. The CEO mind is quiet and peaceful, able to focus on the present moment, thinking only of the task at hand. In addition, if you find yourself in a meeting fighting for your own position, with your only goal being to win the argument, these thoughts are from your elephant. Your CEO, by contrast, is interested in a bigger picture, including the opposite point of view that can be integrated into a solution.

Another quality of the elephant is instant reaction. Neuroscience tells us that the mind reacts in a small fraction of a second, especially to things it doesn't like. The instant reaction causes problems when it displays negative emotion, such as anger or impatience. Your CEO is patient and slower to respond, taking time to formulate a wise response rather than act instantly out of fear or protective self-interest. Moreover, psychologist Jonathan Haidt said that everyone has a "Like-o-meter" in their head that is constantly analyzing things for what it likes and dislikes. Right now you are likely judging what you read in this article. The elephant makes decisions based on personal like and dislike toward people or tasks. The CEO, on the other hand,

Inner Elephant	Inner CEO
Monkey mind	Quiet mind
Own view	Bigger picture
Reactive	Thoughtful response
Judgmental	Cause and Effect
Find Fault	Open, Appreciative
Feel Resistance	In the Flow

TABLE 1

"I do not understand my own actions."

detaches from personal likes and dislikes and seeks a balanced view of underlying cause-effect relationships as a basis for action.

The elephant is always scanning the environment for threats, and hence is in a mind-set of finding fault, and of resisting things it dislikes. *Negativity bias* is the term used in psychology to describe how our minds are tuned to perceive bad things more readily than good things. Evolutionary psychologists say this quality was originally a protection against predators. The inner CEO, by contrast, is able to stay open-minded, and sees people, events, and even problems through a lens of thankfulness and appreciation for whatever positive benefit they contain. Likewise, the elephant will resist, postpone, and procrastinate when facing an unwanted task, such as a needed personal confrontation, while the inner CEO feels less fear and is able to flow into and through these tasks with little hesitation.

How to Start Leading Yourself

Recognizing the two parts is a step toward building up the CEO part of your brain. The next step is to practice using the CEO rather than the older elephant circuitry. Indeed, your elephant needs direction from your CEO to overcome its natural tendency toward overreaction, impulsiveness, procrastination, or lack of focus. The elephant thoughts stored in the brain often produce a poor leader. In other words, a residue of responses from early life conditioning may detract from an effective leadership response right now. Things go better for leaders when their inner CEO is the master and the elephant is the servant. For example, Carol Bartz, CEO of Yahoo, had a bad habit of interrupting before people could finish a sentence.

She had to teach herself to take a breath, to shut up and listen. The first managerial job for Alan Mullaly, CEO of Ford, was as an engineering supervisor. His tendency to oversupervise led him to require people to show him their work, over and over again. When engineers started to quit, Mullaly changed his perspective, learned to communicate a bigger picture of mission and purpose, and encouraged those under him to be in more control of their work. Like Mullaly and Bartz, most leaders know *what* they should be doing differently. But changing yourself is not easy.

Here are some techniques to strengthen your inner CEO to have more control over your elephant's thinking and behavior. These techniques require some deliberate practice. Choose a technique that resonates for you and practice it several times to create a new groove in the CEO circuitry of your brain.

- *Calm down.* Remember, an agitated elephant is harder to control than a calm elephant. Anger, fear, frustration, and craving all give the elephant more power, so calm down before making a decision or pushing the e-mail send button. If you are procrastinating, your elephant is feeling low-level anxiety. The inner elephant is easier to manage when you are relaxed. For example, if you are procrastinating, relax rather than trying to force yourself into the task. Take three deep breaths or just sit by your task until the feeling of resistance passes. Sitting quietly by the task will calm you down, and soon you will reach out and start to work productively.

Instant reaction causes problems when it displays negative emotion.

Get everything you are doing out of your head and written down on paper.

- *Ask yourself questions.* Deepak Chopra, celebrity self-help guru, teaches a leadership course at Northwestern's Kellogg Business School and recently was ordained as a Buddhist monk. The long hours of prayer, meditation, and reflection changed the way he teaches. He now counsels his clients to spend some time each day working on questions such as "What's my purpose in life?" and "What kind of contribution do I want to make to my business?" Other questions could include, "What am I feeling right now?" "What is my mood?" "What is my purpose in doing this activity?" "What outcome do I really want?" The secret to these questions is their inward focus, which is the province of the CEO part of the brain. The inner CEO can see your thoughts and what is happening within your mind and body, while the elephant brain is designed to sense the external world through the five senses. Reflecting inwardly may feel a little strange at first, but will strengthen your CEO.

- *STOP.* This acronym is a reminder to periodically stop for a moment to *Step back, Think, Organize* your thoughts, and then *Proceed.* One manager taped STOP to the crystal of her wristwatch so she would be reminded of it several times a day. STOP allows you to periodically detach from your elephant. Perhaps take a breath, clear your head, take a look around, gather yourself, and then proceed from your CEO awareness. Earlier in his career, Richard Anderson, CEO of Delta Airlines, learned to stop himself before he lost his temper when he realized he was setting the wrong tone for his organization. Breaking the anger habit was vital because everything he did as the leader was an example to those around him.

- *Review the day.* Spend 10 minutes each evening reviewing the behaviors that worked and did not work during the day. To make sure you take the time to adopt this practice, schedule this activity in a quiet place and at the same time each night. At first it is hard to remember anything that happened, but with practice you will remember everything. Think about the positive CEO-type behaviors and review the negative elephant-type occurrences. As you replay incidents in your mind, you will discover more of the desired behavior repeating itself the next day while the undesired behavior will appear less often until it ultimately disappears.

- *Consult with others.* Consulting with just one person before making a decision or taking action will enlarge your elephant's thinking beyond its typical small and one-sided viewpoint. Consult with several people and your perspective will become large and balanced. Try consulting on every large or small decision for one day and witness the perspectives that emerge. Break free of the elephant's desire to believe that its own answers are always better. There is a dual benefit to consulting with others. By practicing this routine you engage others in decision making and you expand your own wisdom.

- *Slow down your reactions.* A busy manager under pressure may react too strongly to a problem. Practice a new response pattern, such as counting to 10, waiting a minute, or waiting 24 hours, and you will soon stop overreacting. A senior executive at an auto supply company learned to always ignore his "response 1" to bad news and wait for his "response 2," even if it meant responding the next day after sleeping on the topic. His response 2 was always wiser than his initial reaction. Jeffery Katzenberg installed a five-second delay on his reactions so others could express their views first. After deciding he didn't have to always be right,

His ex-wife soon inquired, "Where did your anger go?"

Katzenberg found that the five-second delay enabled a more robust and effective dialogue in his meetings.

- *Create a mental picture.* Visualizing a desired behavior in your mind has a powerful impact on your elephant. Spend a moment imagining how you want to give a speech, or handle a difficult conversation, and you will provide a vivid visual instruction to your elephant. Sports psychology research shows that mental rehearsal often is as effective as physical practice for improving performance. Take a few minutes to repeatedly visualize doing a dreaded task, and you will more calmly and smoothly flow through it.

- *Talk to yourself.* The practice of mentally talking to yourself in an intentional and structured way may be the hidden treasure of self-management. Offering an instruction to your elephant in the form of a well-crafted autosuggestion tells the elephant what it needs to change. Repeating something like "I am appreciating others more," or "I am listening more carefully," or "I am delegating more responsibility," or "I am becoming more organized" twenty times morning and evening and during breaks (while driving or exercising) typically produces a noticeable change within a few days. If used extensively this type of self-talk can even reprogram a deeply held aspect of self-image or way of thinking.

- *Provide a structure.* Go to a fat camp for two weeks and you will miraculously find yourself exercising and eating a healthy diet every day until you return home. Why? The camp provides a specific structure for spending your time. Inner elephants also respond to explicit and detailed instructions from the inner executive. Therefore, get everything you are doing out of your head and written down on paper, and write down key steps and a deadline for each task. Psychologists call highly specific written steps "implementation intentions." This detailed structure makes it easier for your elephant to comply.

- *Try meditation.* Meditation quiets the active or racing mind and can awaken a deep sense of happiness. A good way to meditate is to focus your attention on an anchor object or phrase. Focus on watching your breathing or slowly repeat a word or phrase that has meaning for you. David Lynch, a director whose films include *Lost Highway* and *Mulholland Drive,* started practicing Transcendental Meditation (focus on repeating a mantra for 20 minutes twice a day). His ex-wife soon inquired, "Where did your anger go?" Lynch's anger had disappeared and was replaced with deep creativity and feelings of well-being. He still meditates twice a day 30 years later. Meditation is not for everyone. If it appeals to you, then it is important to find an approach that feels right. A good book for beginners is *The Relaxation Response* by Herbert Benson.

If you are not fulfilling your leadership potential, it may be because of a faulty habit or behavior stored in the elephant part of your brain. With practice, you can correct many shortcomings as your inner CEO becomes ascendant and takes control. You will see a change in your approach to being a leader. As you practice, you may see general signs of progress such as more self-discipline, less worry, a calm and deliberate approach, more listening and less telling, increased executive presence and focus, and concern for the long term rather than wanting everything right now.

The trick is to lead yourself first to become a first-rate leader of other people. As you find yourself more in the flow, with your rough edges softening and your faulty behaviors falling away, you are becoming the best leader that lies within you. Others will respond to the new you. Moreover, greater insight into yourself leads to greater insight into other people. You likely will begin to notice the elephant and executive within other people. With the broader perspective, patience, and grace of your inner CEO, you may find yourself passing along your wisdom to others as you coach them to lead through their inner CEO.

Richard L. Daft is the author of "The Executive and the Elephant: A Leader's Guide for Building Inner Excellence." As the Brownlee O. Currey, Jr. Professor of Management at Vanderbilt University's Owen Graduate School of Management, he teaches and coaches executives and MBA students on leadership and self-management. He has written 13 books, including his best-selling textbooks on management and leadership, and is listed as one of the most highly cited professors in the fields of business and economics.

MANAGING UP THE GENERATIONAL LADDER

Larry and Meagan Johnson

In an AARP survey published in May 2008, 27 percent of workers ages 45 and up said the economic slowdown had prompted them to postpone plans to retire. The good news for employers is that Boomers will continue to be in the workforce for some time to come. The bad news for Gen X and Gen Y is that Boomers will continue to be in the workforce for some time to come, which may impede upward movement for the younger generation. In many organizations, however, especially those with a technology bent, Gen Xers and Yers are getting promoted anyway—and find themselves managing Boomers who are old enough to be their parents.

While this can potentially be an awkward position for leaders to find themselves in, it is actually a great opportunity to tap into a wealth of experience and knowledge. We have found four key ways that younger leaders can maximize the productivity and contributions of these older men and women who report to them. First, younger leaders need to find interesting ways to get older workers engaged and to contribute their considerable experience, knowledge, and perspective. Second, younger leaders have to find ways to show Boomers that they are willing to work hard to earn the loyalty of their elders. Third, they must be smart about and sensitive to what motivates older workers to perform, produce, and excel. Finally, the fourth key to managing up is to be creative and figure out ways to tailor one's management approach to the very distinct working styles and preferences of older workers.

Leverage Boomers' Experience

All of us like to think we have value. To a Boomer, much of that value comes from having decades of experience. Acknowledge that experience by asking for advice. Be careful, however, not to come across as pandering to older people. Most people can tell when managers say something they don't really mean. Focus on the work, and ask legitimate questions that acknowledge the older person's experience.

Assigning them to be mentors is a good way to do this. Many Japanese companies do this by creating a system of *sempai-kohai*. A promising young manager, the *kohai* (which literally means "junior") is assigned to an older, more experienced manager, the *sempai* (which means "senior" or "mentor"). The *sempai* is usually outside the *kohai*'s chain of command and functions much like a godparent to the *kohai*. The *sempai*'s role involves helping the *kohai* succeed in all areas of work, from technical questions to operational issues to organizational politics. The process offers obvious benefits to the *kohai* cohort as well as to the organization, but it also honors the *sempai* cohort for their institutional knowledge and wisdom. For many Boomers, the opportunity to act as a mentor can keep them interested in the job when their thoughts are wandering toward retirement and golf.

Of course, asking carefully selected Boomers to function as your *sempai* can not only show your appreciation for their experience, it can help you steer clear of organizational pitfalls. All great leaders surround themselves with advisers who may have wisdom in areas they lack. Smart second lieutenants in the field of battle will do the same with their veteran sergeants, who may lack their officers' education and training but do have the experience that will help keep both officer and unit alive. Making an ally of a Boomer who holds the respect of the team will do the same for you. Finding and partnering with a master sergeant will enhance your credibility with the entire team and get you the support you need when things get rough. Best of all, the Boomer with whom you build this kind of relationship will tend to feel more vested in your success and in the success of the group.

Prove Yourself Worthy

You may well be thinking, "I have no problem respecting their experience, but how do I get them to respect mine?" Answer: accept the reality that, for a while, you will be perceived as "just a kid." You will gain respect based on your performance, your willingness to work hard, your humility, and your ability to do a terrific job. For example, a brilliant young software engineer we know was promoted to lead a team of senior scientists because they were working with advanced systems in which he had expertise. When a disagreement would arise about how to handle a problem with the system, he made it a practice to ask for their opinions first. If their solutions seemed right to him, he'd say something like, "Great, that makes sense to me." If he disagreed,

Most people can tell when managers say something they don't really mean.

he would often make a comment like, "I'm the one with the least experience, so I may be wrong here, but I have an idea. What do you think about . . . " and then present his case. As the Boomers got to know him and to trust that he really understood what he was talking about, he was able to drop the qualifiers and engage with them as equals.

You can also prove yourself by superbly fulfilling the tasks of your leadership role that ensure the Boomers get what they need to do their jobs well. You may remember Radar O'Reilly, the cute, naive company clerk and bugler from the popular television series *M*A*S*H*. His real job, however, was to get the surgeons and nurses what they needed to do their jobs well. If they needed scalpels, he tracked them down and delivered them. If they needed a generator but none was available, he'd wheel and deal with clerks from other units to score one. When you are a manager of people older than yourself, their view of you as doing a great job in your role as leader is essential. This is especially true when they observe how you deal with the "suits" upstairs. If you do this well—and get them what they need to do their jobs well—their respect for you will climb.

This Radar O'Reilly management approach also includes making sure your people continue to get the training and updating they need. Neglecting the growth needs of Boomers is understandable. They seem to be successful doing what they are doing, so why would they need training? After all, they'll be leaving soon, so why waste money developing them when it can be better spent on someone younger?

When you are a manager of people older than yourself, their view of you as doing a great job is essential.

That can be a mistake, because, as the AARP survey indicates, many Boomers aren't planning to leave any time soon, so they will be applying the skills they acquire for some time to come. And if some Boomers retire before you get a full return on your investment, you may be able to recover it with some creative planning.

We know a 65-year-old telecommunications engineer who oversaw the installation of phone systems for large corporate customers. Six months before her retirement, her company significantly upgraded these systems, which required extensive new training for installers and the completion of a certification process. Her boss made a deal with her: He would send her to the training so she could be certified if she would agree to be on call for one year after her retirement. Not only that, but she would be brought in at her regular salary, prorated to a daily fee. It was a win-win. The company received the benefit of her certification for the last months she was there, plus a full year of her services as an on-call contractor. She received the benefit of being able to charge other consulting clients more after she retired because she had this certification. And what about the younger boss? He got her loyalty, respect, motivation, and cooperation.

Whether or not you can work such a sweet deal with your Boomers, it would serve you well to think twice before automatically writing them off for training, no matter how close they are to leaving.

Motivate Them on Their Terms

Like any generation, Boomers like to be recognized for their achievements. To the degree you can make that happen, you will reap the rewards of their loyalty. If you are more than 10 years younger than the Boomer you are praising, see if you can enlist the help of another Boomer from whom the praise will carry more meaning. For example, during a team meeting, Judy, the Gen Y team leader, said to Jack, the Boomer, "Bill was telling me about what a great job you did on the Anderson account—right, Bill?" At that point, Bill made a comment supporting Jack's achievement. It gave Jack a double dose of praise, and it built Judy's credibility because she did her homework and also proved herself willing to give credit where credit is due.

It also pays to know each of the people you are recognizing, and tailor your praise to their needs. We were speaking at a conference of Harley-Davidson dealers where the owners of one dealership told us this story: For his loyalty and dedication, the owners wanted to do something special for their lead mechanic, a Boomer who had been with them for 20 years. They decided to give him and his wife an all-expenses-paid vacation to Hawaii. At a special luncheon, unbeknownst to the mechanic, they described his stellar performance over the years and then awarded him the trip.

From the look on his face, they could tell he was not thrilled about the award. Later, they asked him what he thought of the trip. He replied that he didn't mean to be ungrateful, but his wife had recently left him for another man, and he didn't particularly want to go to Hawaii with her or anyone else. The flabbergasted

Give credit where credit is due.

owners asked him what he would prefer instead, and he said he really liked the fancy toolbox the Snap-on sales representative had tried to sell him recently. The owners offered the toolbox instead of the Hawaii trip, and the mechanic felt better—not great—but better. It would have been better to check with him before the public ceremony.

What motivates people is highly individualistic, especially for Boomers who have lived long enough to have a wealth of experiences. In choosing special awards or incentives for them, increased contributions to a 401(K), flexible schedules so they can start developing postretirement interests, and opportunities to be recognized and applauded for their achievements make sense for most, but that doesn't mean all Boomers will want those things.

The obvious step is to ask the Boomer what reward would best recognize the contribution you wish to honor—and then listen. For example, a Generation X manager wants to reward a Boomer employee for good work, so she offers him some time off to spend with his family. He declines, noting that he has a big project he's trying to complete and taking time off would just add to his stress. The smart manager would ask, "How can I reward you for your terrific work?"

Vary Your Approach

In the past 25 years, participative management has gained a great deal of popularity. Savvy managers have learned that soliciting employee input into the decision-making process raises the odds they will make better decisions and that their decisions will have greater support from the employees affected by it. Does that approach always work? Of course not. Sometimes it's a terrible approach that only frustrates people.

For example, we are fervent proponents of participative management—both as leaders and when we work for someone else. We want the boss to *ask* for our input before making a decision. A few years ago, however, while on a family whitewater rafting trip, we discovered that sometimes we just want to be told what to do. We all had paddles and were expected to row in sync forward or back-

From the look on his face, they could tell he was not thrilled about the award.

ward to steer the boat. The guide, who was acting as our manager that day, sat in the back and shouted the orders: "Right side forward, left side back . . . left side forward, right side back," and so on. As we raced through the rapids, the orders came quickly as we dodged boulders and tree trunks at breakneck speed.

This was not the time for our guide to ask for our input on which direction we should paddle. We did not want, nor need, participative management—we wanted and needed to be told what to do. Luckily, he was good at that. Later, around the campfire, as we discussed the next day's journey, the guide asked us for input on seating arrangements in the raft, how we'd like to time the breaks, and what we'd like to have for lunch. He stepped out of the telling mode and into the asking mode—and we appreciated his ability to do both.

Younger managers will be well served to vary their interaction style with older employees to match employees' needs at the time. For example, suppose an older employee doesn't understand how to manage the company's internal social networking system and figures asking for help would look foolish. If the younger manager's style is to assume the older one should know how to do it (Gee, doesn't everybody get Facebook?) anything the younger manager says about using social networking is going to fall on deaf ears. On the other hand, a younger manager who is sensitive to the older employee's dilemma might schedule some private time

Every generation adds value to an organization.

to walk the employee through the process, or solicit the help of another older employee who understands social networking to help the employee while minimizing his embarrassment.

Sensitivity to the other person's needs and a willingness to adjust your approach are keys to success here.

The Bottom Line

Every generation adds value to an organization. Boomers may be nearing retirement, but that doesn't mean they should be shunted to the side and ignored. They have the experience that can provide historical perspective for the decisions you face. They have overcome many obstacles, and that kind of tenacity can help your organization meet new challenges. They are team players who can enhance any group in which they participate.

But they need to be engaged. They need to feel they are still valuable to the organization. They need the freedom to act on their accumulated knowledge and skills without being micromanaged—but they don't want to be left totally adrift.

Successfully managing Boomers means keeping them motivated and excited about their jobs—communicating and listening—to ensure that they are aligned with the goals of your group and organization, and giving them the support they need to continue to perform at the highest levels. Younger managers can do this if they are careful to prove themselves worthy of managing Boomers by making sure that Boomers get what they need to make the last years of their employment successful.

Larry and Meagan Johnson, a father-daughter team, are the Johnson Training Group (www .johnsontraininggroup.com). Their clients include American Express, Harley-Davidson, Nordstrom, Dairy Queen, and many others. They are leading experts on corporate culture and managing multigenerational workplaces, and are coauthors of "Generations, Inc.: From Boomers to Linksters—Managing the Friction Between Generations at Work."

BUILDING HIGH-TRUST ORGANIZATIONS

Pamela S. Shockley-Zalabak and Sherwyn P. Morreale

Most leaders would agree that high levels of trust are critically important to the success of their organizations and businesses. Trust is fundamental for bottom-line results. Numerous studies link trust and perceptions of integrity to economic performance. Restaurants, sales forces, NCAA teams, and a host of other organizations all perform better when trust levels are high. A 2005 Russell Investment Group report showed that *Fortune* magazine's "100 Best Companies to Work For"—in which trust comprises 60 percent of the criteria—earned more than four times the returns of the broader market over the prior seven years. A PricewaterhouseCoopers study of corporate innovation among the *Financial Times* 100 showed that the number one differentiating factor between the top innovators and the bottom innovators was trust. Evidence exists linking trust to the ability to create adaptive organizations, form strategic alliances, and work in effective virtual teams. Why?

The answer is simple. Important organizational knowledge never resides only at the top. If we cannot delegate with confidence, we create costly redundancy and reporting structures that lower efficiency. When we can't trust, then autonomous rapid response is impossible. Problems are not solved, opportunities are missed, costs rise, and effectiveness suffers. Conversely, creativity, innovation, and ambiguity offer major organizational opportunities. For creativity and innovation to flourish, people at all organizational levels must have the motivation to challenge conventional wisdom and push to change the status quo. Not surprisingly, creativity and innovation are likely to flourish in climates of trust and shut down when distrust is prevalent.

Unfortunately, distrust occurs more easily than trust in many organizations and relationships. If I do not trust you, I have no surprises, no need to feel vulnerable, and no disappointments. I may feel disgust when you break your word, but I won't feel betrayed because I expected you to fail me. Distrusting relationships are characterized by low interdependence: I simply won't depend on you because I don't think I can, and I don't want you depending on me. I don't listen to your ideas because I don't expect them to be worth anything. I don't expect you to produce anything of special worth, and I would not believe it if you did. Chances are we will never work together very effectively.

This distrust contributes to "us versus them" behavior. I know my group is producing, but other groups aren't. We won't share how we solved the problem because we will look better if we win. You can't trust others to give credit where it is due, and since it is hard enough to trust those immediately around me, don't ask me to trust people I don't know.

Leaders clearly know such distrust lowers employee desire to contribute to productivity goals and breeds fear and a host of other destructive behaviors. But they often don't realize how expensive it is. The U.S. Sarbanes-Oxley Act with its myriad of financial compliance obligations costs money and is fundamentally related to breaches of trust. The Act mandates monitoring and surveillance systems, highly prescriptive contracts, extensive rules and regulations, low supervisor-to-employee ratios, and a host of other organizational processes requiring substantial resources both human and financial. We are not arguing that distrust always is wrong, but that it is fundamentally more expensive than trust.

To address the challenge of distrust, the model for trust building in organizations we now present is both research based and practice driven; it is designed to produce the staying power that only trust can generate. This model is designed to help leaders establish clear yet ambitious performance goals, resulting in superb execution while stimulating creativity and innovation for the future. Yes, we believe trust is *the main thing*, the underlying and necessary foundation of organizational success.

The Organizational Trust Model

The research we conducted for our book, *Building the High-Trust Organization: Strategies for Supporting Five Key Dimensions of Trust*, supported a model of organizational trust with five key drivers:

- Competence
- Openness and honesty
- Concern for employees and stakeholders
- Reliability
- Identification

Our research team learned that these five drivers were strong and stable predictors of organizational trust across cultures, languages, industries, and types of organizations. The more positive the trust scores of an organization on our Organizational Trust Inventory,

I won't feel betrayed because I expected you to fail me.

the more effective the organization was perceived to be and the more satisfied with their jobs employees were. Conversely, lower trust scores predicted lower effectiveness and less job satisfaction. In other words, positive evaluations of each of the five drivers predict that an organization will receive overall high trust scores, while negative evaluations of the five dimensions result in low trust. Let's now take a closer look at the five drivers or dimensions of trust and consider some strategies leaders can use to promote them in their organizations.

Dimension One: Competence

The competence dimension is the ability of the organization, through its leaders' strategies, decision making, and other capabilities, to meet the challenges of its environment. Competence relates to the overall efficiency of the organization as well as to capabilities of employees at all organizational levels. Competence involves the extent to which we see not only our coworkers and leaders as effective, but also our organization as a whole. Competence reflects how strongly we believe our organization will compete and survive in whatever situation or setting we find ourselves in. Finally, competence is measured by an organization's ability to achieve its objectives.

Leader Strategies for Building Trust in Competence

Purpose, vision, leadership, goals, strategy, structure, and execution all contribute to competence and perceptions of competence. However, it is important to understand that being a competent leader and having others trust in your competence is not the same thing. Being competent is fundamental, but having others *trust* in that competence is equally important. It is relatively easy to believe that trust in the competence of an organization contributes significantly to the success of sales, marketing, goal achievement, and customer or client satisfaction. Customer, donor, and client loyalty are critical ingredients of long-term positive results.

What is not as readily understood is that trust in the competence of an organization actually contributes to the competence of the organization. High-quality potential employees, donors, customers, and clients are attracted to organizations they believe are on the leading edge, get results, are innovative, and have bright futures. High-quality stakeholders have choices with quality. They choose organizations in which they trust the competence of leaders and their ability to frame a vision and set goals and strategy in pursuit of that vision. Additionally, current employees are more innovative when they believe their ideas will meet with a fair and competent evaluation. Both employees and external stakeholders exhibit more loyalty to organizations with track records for competence.

Strategies for building trust in competence begin with understanding the current state of competence in the organization and the evaluation of that competence by stakeholders. Core competence must be addressed at all levels and continuous development made part of both

Distrust is not always wrong, but it is fundamentally more expensive than trust.

Trust in the competence of an organization contributes to the competence of the organization.

leader and employee evaluations. Next, leaders must pay attention to purpose and vision. The third key strategy is a comprehensive and sometimes difficult assessment of the quality of leaders themselves. Leaders and managers design the processes that produce the results of the organization—whether the results are good or bad. Leaders build trust when they focus directly on hiring and promoting people who exhibit competence. Trust in competence rests on understanding the core capabilities of an organization and working continuously to address weaknesses and get better. Trust is built when problems are solved quickly and with quality. Product and service excellence are fundamental for trust. Leaders build trust when they commit to continually improving and developing a culture of competence. Finally, a leading mark of competence is the ability to identify, plan, communicate, and execute needed change.

Dimension Two: Openness and Honesty

The openness and honesty dimension is reflected in how organizations communicate about problems, engage in constructive disagreements, and provide input into job-related decisions. Openness and honesty are evaluated positively when managers and supervisors

Leaders build trust when they commit to a culture of competence.

keep confidences and provide information about job performance and evaluation of performance. Employees evaluate an organization as open and honest when they are provided information about how job-related problems are handled and how major organizational decisions will affect them as individuals. Making long-term strategic direction available to all employees is a mark of an open and honest organization. Openness and honesty seem straightforward and certainly related to trust. However, over 80 percent of all surveyed organizations report communication problems, with credibility of leadership communication generally rated low.

Leader Strategies for Building Trust in Openness and Honesty

Trust in openness and honesty improves the ability of an organization to collaborate, partner with others, and execute day-to-day strategy. This is not hard to understand. If I trust you to be open and honest with me, I am significantly more likely to be open and honest with you. I will share information, and that sharing contributes to enhanced creativity and innovation. Open and honest communication reduces uncertainty—I know where I stand, and I know where you stand. We can engage in constructive disagreement. Reduction of uncertainty and the ability to collaborate engender more loyalty and satisfaction with all aspects of work.

Accurate information is fundamental to trust building, as are explanations for decisions and a general openness and timeliness in all communication behaviors. For immediate supervisors, information flow, including adequate explanations and timely feedback on deci-

sions, has the strongest relationship with trust in the supervisor. Both managers and supervisors who freely exchange thoughts and ideas with others enhance overall perceptions of trust. The organization is described as transparent with high trust levels.

We are convinced building trust in openness and honesty is based on adopting a "need to share" instead of a "need to know" strategy and mentality throughout the organization, including leaders, employees, and significant stakeholders. A "need to share" is not one-way communication. Rather, it involves processes and practices that create sharing of knowledge, ideas, issues, or problems throughout the organization and with external stakeholders. Leaders need to engage in comprehensive assessment of the current state of openness and honesty throughout the organization. Communication practices must be understood with particular emphasis on the communication excellence of leaders. Finally, a comprehensive organizational communication plan is central to trust-building efforts.

Dimension Three: Concern for Employees and Stakeholders

The concern for employees dimension is squarely about communication and employment practices. For employees to trust that the organization has concern for them, they need to believe they are heard. It begins with the immediate supervisor or manager listening to employees and acting on their needs, ideas, or concerns. Trust is related to leaders' attempts to bring information to employees and to how leaders talk about any specific employee group to others. The concern dimension is reflected in the perception and reality of top management wanting to communicate regularly with employees and exhibiting a willingness to hear and act on their concerns. Employees trust the organization when they believe their immediate supervisors or managers are concerned about their personal well-being. Top management is trusted when policies and procedures within the organization reflect concern for the well-being of employees generally. Safety procedures, health plans and benefits, family leave, vacation, performance evaluation, salary scales, promotional practices, and a host of other organization-wide processes determine whether employees trust the organization to have concern for their well-being.

Trust in concern for stakeholders is directly related to employee satisfaction and perceptions of overall organizational effectiveness. Employees are retained at a higher rate when they trust their organizations to be concerned for their welfare. And employees are more productive when they believe they are working in an organization that cares about their well-being. Customers, clients, or supporters are more loyal to organizations that care about their needs, whether for quality products and services, meeting societal needs, or for timely response to problems. Stakeholders, including customers and clients, also tend to evaluate concern based on service support, pricing, product or service quality, dispute-resolution policies, timeliness, and overall ease and accessibility of interacting with the organization.

Leader Strategies for Building Trust in Concern for Employees and Stakeholders

Building trust in concern for stakeholders is based on a genuine caring for others, a commitment to doing what is right, and a belief that caring and commitment will generate organizational excellence. However, building trust in concern is more than leader intent. It is the continual examination of communications, policies, practices, and processes for the concern and caring they reflect. It is aligning intent with action and developing an understanding of how stakeholders evaluate the impact of action.

Leaders build trust in stakeholder concern by first understanding how stakeholders perceive the current state of the organization's concern for them. Policies and practices such as hiring, performance appraisal, salary administration, promotion practices, and grievance processes all are related to expressions of concern and caring. Customers, clients, volunteers, or donors base trust evaluations on organizational interactions ranging from service support to return policies. A comprehensive understanding of policies and practices goes beyond the most obvious to include conflict resolution, financial controls, reward and recognition programs, medical benefits, leave policies, and a host of other potential areas of concern.

Open and honest communication reduces uncertainty.

High-trust organizations excel at communicating their concern for stakeholders by continuously aligning actual practice with communication efforts.

Dimension Four: Reliability

The reliability dimension is about leaders, supervisors, and managers keeping commitments and maintaining basic follow-through. It is about telling all organizational members when something has to change and why. It is consistent behavior from day to day. For top management, reliability is keeping commitments made to the organization and telling the organization the reason if any commitments must change. The reliability dimension of trust should not be confused with staying the same or the status quo. Reliability is doing what we say we are going to do and saying why. Often that means communicating about the need for change from the status quo. Reliability also is consistently listening to ideas, issues, and concerns. It is responding to others on a regular basis, whether the response is positive or negative. Reliability is a steadiness in behavior that builds the trust necessary for uncertain times. A reliable organization is a trusted organization.

Leader Strategies for Building Trust in Reliability

Trust in reliability comes from both individual and macroorganizational experiences. Employees determine whether their supervisors follow through with what they say they are going to do. They watch to see whether or not their supervisors behave consistently from day to day. Trust in top leaders is based in part on evaluations of whether or not individuals at the top keep their commitments to employees and other important stakeholders. High trust in organizational reliability promotes employee satisfaction and perceptions of organizational effectiveness. High trust in reliability assists organizations in working through crises and problems. When crises and problems arise, stakeholders trust, based on prior experiences, that the reliable organization has the ability to meet present challenges.

To build trust in reliability, leaders must not only understand their own reliability profile, they must also understand the profile throughout the organization. Words and actions must be aligned to develop a culture of reliability. Next, accountability for results is fundamental for reliability. Promoting accountability requires examining performance expectations for top leaders and determining how those expectations are met and translated into expectations throughout the organization. All employees should be able to identify how their performance fits into the overall results expectations of the organization. Promoting accountability requires support for individuals who take responsibility, regardless of their job positions. Blame is avoided, which encourages individuals to admit mistakes, offer solutions to problems, and work for positive change beyond their specific job duties. Finally, an organization that promotes accountability has leaders who are transparent, who take personal responsibility for results, and who provide inclusive credit for high performance.

Dimension Five: Identification

The identification dimension is the connection between the organization and individual employees, most often based on core values. Identification relates to an individual establishing a personal connection with management and peers and, in a more subtle way, with the entire organization. Identification comes when individuals believe their values are reflected in the values the organization exhibits in day-to-day behaviors. It is not surprising that identification or the lack thereof often is directly related to the quality of management-employee relationships. Employees identify with and trust organizations if the organization conducts itself in a way closely related to the way employees believe the organization should operate. It

Trust stops fear in its tracks.

is readily apparent that geographically dispersed workers who have little interpersonal contact with management may be challenged to identify with the organization. The importance of identification for trust requires new thinking about trust building in a global environment.

Leader Strategies for Building Trust in Identification

Organizations do not enjoy strong identification when their competence, openness and honesty, concern for stakeholders, or reliability are in question. However, identification requires experiences beyond those surrounding these four drivers. Stakeholders experience strong identification with organizations when they share values and purpose and experience connection to organizational members, services, and products. Not surprisingly, strong identification fosters quality and is related to employee and external satisfaction with the organization and perceptions of effectiveness. Strong identification has additional benefits. Experience with our clients and extensive research support our view that strong organizational identification helps individuals cope during times of uncertainty. Trust in the values of an organization provides stakeholders the bonding it takes to work through difficulties. Loyalty resulting from strong identification actually buys time for leaders to deal with problems.

A strategy for assessing how stakeholders identify with an organization is as important as assessments of the other drivers. Understanding the norms and values of the culture of the organization, and the extent to which all stakeholders identify with those norms and values, is critical to building trust through identification. In addition, policies and practices, along with a communication plan about those organizational processes, also contribute to organizational identification. Excelling at communicating values, trust, and connections to the organization to all stakeholders is a leadership responsibility.

Final Thoughts: Trust Is the Main Thing

The challenges to trust are daunting. Our global environment complicates trust building. Cultural differences inhibit collaboration, and we must work beyond our limitations. Trust in global alliances is influenced by trust in governments, legal protections, and institutional operations not dependent on personal familiarity or similarity. Trust becomes the core of our virtual work environments.

We believe the five drivers of trust provide concrete guidance for leaders who wish to focus on trust in complex and changing environments. Trust is fundamental to stimulate the innovation, creativity, and risk taking needed to bring about productive change. We hope we have made the case: *High organizational trust transforms individuals and entire organizations for the better.* Therefore, trust building is a primary imperative for leaders. Trust is not—as some would have us believe—a nice but elusive concept unsuited for a turbulent, uncertain, rapidly changing, and often frightening world. Trust is the bond and stimulant that produces lasting and excellent results. Trust replaces the need for certainty and control as our bridge to the future. Trust stops fear in its tracks. We have choices. The choice to build trust is practical and will bring measurable and positive success. The choice to build trust also speaks to the best in all of us, our high ideals, and our dreams for the future. We hope you will lead with trust as the *main thing.*

Pamela S. Shockley-Zalabak is chancellor and a professor of communication at the University of Colorado at Colorado Springs. She is the coauthor of "Building the High-Trust Organization: Strategies for Supporting Five Key Dimensions of Trust" (with Sherwyn Morreale and Michael Z. Hackman), as well as six other books and more than 100 articles and productions on organizational communication. Prior to assuming her chancellor responsibilities, she was vice chancellor for student success and founding chair of the UCCS Communication Department. Shockley-Zalabak also is President of Communi-Con, Inc., a consulting organization working with clients in the United States, Europe, and Asia and is the producer of award-winning television documentaries aired nationally and in major U.S. markets.

Sherwyn P. Morreale is an associate professor and director of graduate studies in communication at the University of Colorado at Colorado Springs. She is the author of three communication textbooks and numerous articles and chapters for collected volumes and special monographs in the communication discipline. From 1997 to 2006, Morreale served as associate director of the National Communication Association, the oldest and largest association of professors in the communication discipline in the world.

MOVING UP: TEN QUESTIONS FOR LEADERS IN TRANSITION (PART II)

Robert Bruce Shaw and Michael M. Chayes

In the last issue of *Leader to Leader* (*No. 59*, Winter 2011) we discussed the four stages of a successful transition into a new leadership role, with a focus on an initial "discovery" phase. The first task of an incoming leader is to learn about his or her new business, organization, and people—keeping an open mind and truly testing assumptions about what is needed moving forward. In this issue, we discuss the questions that each new leader will need to answer in the remaining three transitional stages:

- *Define:* Mapping out key priorities and strategies.

- *Deliver:* Sustaining focus and ensuring progress.

- *Build:* Building productive relationships with stakeholders.

All four stages and their accompanying questions are shown in the sidebar on page 47.

What are your "vital few" areas of focus for the first 12 months?

After spending time learning about the organization in the Discovery phase, the new leader needs to develop a point of view on the "vital few" business priorities and determine how to gain necessary support for the emerging plan. This is not, however, a top-down process as much as it is the development of a shared understanding of the future direction and the leader's broad plan of action. Specifically, the leader will want to provide others with a clear strategic narrative (where we have been as a company, where we are going . . .) and associated set of priorities (fix the core business, grow in emerging markets . . .). Leaders need to sequence the work streams in each of these priority areas to avoid overwhelming their organizations. Moreover, each new leader needs to motivate others to build and implement a shared plan of action. Successful leaders develop the change management skills that allow them to engage important organization members in co-designing and sharing in the change strategy. To be clear, the new leader needs to be directive in some cases, particularly in a turnaround, but should remain open to changing his or her emerging vision, based on additional input and emerging events.

After defining the direction and plan of action, the new leader will want to establish a management process to ensure focus and sufficient progress on the "vital few" priorities. The potential trap for new leaders and their teams is being pulled into a variety of peripheral activities that are not on the critical path to success. The leader can contribute to the problem by attempting to do too much early on (with all the right intentions but with negative results). We recommend that the new leader develop a succinct transition plan that outlines the key priorities for the first six months and periodically check to ensure follow-through in the targeted areas. Leaders may also want to develop a more general one-page summary or road map and a rigorous team review process to assess progress in monthly or quarterly meetings.

Staying Focused on the Vital Few

- Clarify the three or four key areas of focus for your first six months. Also determine how much time, in general, you will need to allocate to

---

TEN QUESTIONS FOR LEADERS IN TRANSITION

Discover (First 30–60 Days; questions reviewed in *Leader to Leader No. 59*)

1. What do you need to learn and how will you learn it?

2. How is the new role different from past roles, and what unique value can you bring to it?

3. What is the carryover from your predecessor and how will it impact you?

4. What lessons from past transitions—your own and others'—are relevant?

Define (Second 30–60 Days)

5. What are your "vital few" areas of focus for the first 12 months?

6. What are the tests and measures by which others will assess you?

Deliver (Remainder of First Year)

7. Which of your leadership behaviors will help, or hinder, in the transition?

8. How will you develop the team needed to deliver on your transition plan?

9. What are the potential derailers for you and your group?

Build (All of first year)

10. Who are your stakeholders and how will you partner with them?

Senior leader transitions are challenging, in part, because they are highly visible.

each of these areas and your high-level tactical actions.

- Identify who you need to engage to "pressure test" and enhance your plan. This list should include those above you in the hierarchy as well as key peers and subordinates.

- Establish how your team will review progress in each of your priority areas (including designation of sponsors on your team for each target area, the data you will use to assess progress, and the frequency of your reviews).

- Periodically, revisit your transition plan to see if any additions or deletions are called for as you become more knowledgeable about the organization or as circumstances change.

What are the tests and measures by which others will assess you?

Transition success means setting the bar above simply meeting short-term business needs or creating positive momentum—though these are important hurdles. Success is more usefully defined as the ability of a new leader, drawing on his or her unique strengths and experience, to establish the conditions for long-term business value creation and growth. While it's in everyone's

interest that transitions result in early wins, the need for speed has to be balanced with the opportunity for long-term payoffs that derive from engaging in a disciplined transition process. This definition of success requires that new leaders develop sufficient knowledge of their organizations and take the time to develop a thoughtful plan to drive future growth. When transitioning leaders adopt a mind-set that includes these strategic success criteria, they enter the transition process with a significant advantage over those whose concept of success is more limited and short-term oriented. That said, the new leader needs to carefully consider the criteria by which he or she will be assessed.

Senior leader transitions are challenging, in part, because they are highly visible. Colleagues use early experiences to judge if a new leader is a good fit for the role and, ultimately, worthy of being followed. Early mistakes are amplified and can quickly derail even the most talented leaders. The exact nature of the tests will vary in each situation, but they are an important dynamic in establishing one's credibility as the new leader. In many cases, the expectations of others are not explicit or are ambiguous in nature, potentially resulting in unfortunate surprises for the new leader as the transition unfolds. This is particularly problematic if the expectations of one's supervisor or Board are unclear. New leaders thus run the risk of failing tests that they don't fully understand or fully appreciate. It is important to consider the nature of these tests, both formal and informal, and identify the most important over the first 6–12 months in a new role.

As consultants, we ask our clients to identify the two or three success metrics on which they will be evaluated (such as meeting revenue targets, demonstrating growth in a critical new market, or resolving outstanding litigation with a key supplier). We also ask new leaders to consider the more informal or softer measures that others, particularly those in positions of authority, will use to assess them. For example, we worked with a new general counsel whose CEO believed that relations with Board members were critical to the new GC's success. The CEO had no formal metrics but said she would know after six months if these relationships were on track.

Defining Your Success Criteria

- Consider the expectations of your key stakeholders (supervisor, customers, direct reports, organizational members) and the lens each will use to assess your performance as a new leader. Also consider what you believe is most important and reconcile any gaps between your views and those of your key stakeholders.

- Identify the two or three core success metrics and the implications of each in terms of where you spend your time and of your overall transition plan.

Which of your leadership behaviors will help, or hinder, in the transition?

During a transition, leaders should compare what they learn about a firm's needs and culture with a candid self-assessment of their own strengths and weaknesses—and come to terms with aspects of the new situation that have the potential to bring out the worst in them. The goal is to identify the capabilities and behaviors needed in the new role and not simply assume that what worked in the past is what is needed moving forward. For example, Elliot Spitzer was by most accounts a very successful New York district attorney and yet a visible failure as governor of New York (for reasons other than those that caused his resignation). In particular, his past had taught him that success comes with taking aggressive positions and overwhelming the opposition. Part of the problem was that he took this leadership model, one that largely worked in his attorney general role, and assumed that it would work in the role of New York governor.

Each leader comes into a role with clear strengths along with potential vulnerabilities. We often find that a leader's strengths, under the stress of transition, are pushed to the point of becoming weaknesses. For example, we worked with one leader who was very controlling in her management style. This was, in part, a factor in her past success because she managed to achieve results through her intelligence, tenacity, and

What worked in the past is not necessarily what is needed moving forward.

attention to detail. However, her style was problematic when she was promoted and given a broader scope of authority. In essence, her style was not scalable. She could not stay on top of the same level of detail in her expanded role and her more senior direct reports did not appreciate being managed so closely. With some difficulty, she was able to develop a style that was a better fit to her new role even though it was unfamiliar to her.

A new leader will want to solicit input from trusted colleagues on what behavior needs to change upon moving into the new role. Typically, there are only one or two areas that need attention, and the new leader should be careful not to take on too much. There is also a risk of inadvertently undermining a needed strength by overcorrecting in the targeted area. A leader who has a bias for action, for example, may be warned by others that the new job will require a more inclusive style. While we find that most leaders don't fundamentally change their preferred style, some will move too far to the other extreme (for example, seek out so much input that that decisions are not made in a timely manner).

Leveraging Strengths and Managing Vulnerabilities

- Identify the two or three strengths that will be most useful to you in your new role. Consider how to fully leverage these strengths (for example, strategic planning skills can be used to help refine the firm's long-term technology plan, which is unclear).

New leaders often don't have a clearly articulated strategy.

- Consider one or two aspects of your leadership style that may be problematic in relation to your new role. Solicit input from those you trust to identify these areas and, in particular, any blind spots that you may have.

- Determine how you will address the potential vulnerabilities, with specific actions you will take in each targeted area.

- Identify a few people who will provide honest feedback on how you are doing in these areas.

How will you develop the team needed to deliver on your transition plan?

The stereotype of a new leader is that he or she has a well-articulated strategy in coming into a new role and quickly cleans house, replacing many of the existing team in order to better advance that plan. We find that new leaders often don't have a clearly articulated strategy but instead have some emerging ideas and a disjointed set of tactics. In addition, we find that most don't move quickly on changing their new teams but instead keep the existing team members in place as they determine the changes that are needed. Some suggest that the most logical approach is to develop one's strategy and then determine if the leadership team has the requisite capabilities to deliver on that strategy. Others suggest that new leaders must "get the right people on the bus" and then develop the strategy. Our experience is that both of these views are too extreme, as strategy

and the staffing of the team occur in a highly iterative manner.

The new leader needs to work to clarify the long-range vision and, at the same time, assess, develop, and staff the talent to further develop and execute the strategy. The key in managing this process is to have a well-articulated talent plan for the senior team. This 12- to 18-month plan, for the leader's use only, outlines the changes needed in the team over time. This plan includes potential hires in targeted areas as well as individuals on the team who need to be further assessed, developed in a current role, moved to a new role, or removed from the organization. The new leader will also want to consider any actions to take in the first six months to develop the group's capabilities or culture. Many leaders make these talent decisions on an ad hoc basis and have no systematic process to improve their team's capabilities and performance. The talent plan should tap the knowledge gained in the initial Discovery phase of the transition and be sequenced in relation to needs and risks facing the organization.

Enhancing the Capabilities of Your Team

- Determine if your leadership team has the talent and drive needed to develop strategies effectively and execute on both a strategic and operational level.

- Outline the changes you want to make in your team over the next 12–18 months (new members that you bring into the team, new roles for existing members, developmental actions for selected members, team development activities, and so on).

- Determine which members will need more coaching and in what areas. Ensure that you dedicate necessary time to these individuals.

What are potential derailers for you and your group?

Every leader has a short list of key factors that could result in limiting his or her impact in a new role or result in outright derailment. These can be larger situational factors (sudden downturn in business, loss of a major contract, product development failures) or more personal factors (alienation of stakeholders whose support is critical to the firm's success). This is particularly important in relation to the execution of the leader's key priorities during the first year.

One of our clients found it useful to periodically consider what would "kill him" (that is, derail his plan and erode his leadership credibility) if it emerged—even low-probability events. While some of these factors are difficult to anticipate, many can be identified, and actions can be taken to prevent them from occurring, or their impact can be mitigated if they do occur. Leaders can also establish mechanisms to track the status of these potential threats. For example, suppose that as a new executive, you are concerned about a specific product development initiative that is critical to your firm's future growth. You have entered your role with limited understanding of the technology being used and, more generally, of the new product development process. As a result, you know that you are vulnerable in this area, but you can take several actions to protect yourself. For instance, you can establish a formal and disciplined review process with the new product team, make sure that clear metrics and milestones are in place to closely track progress and to quickly surface any issues, and identify an external technology expert to coach you in the development process and success factors.

Identifying Key Derailers

* Consider the factors that could jeopardize the achievement of your priorities or, more generally, the overall success of the enterprise.

Understanding the logic and limits of one's formal power is a key to success.

Stakeholder building is not about accumulating personal power.

---

* Prioritize these risks and determine how the top two or three are best addressed through tracking metrics and preventive actions.

* Periodically discuss with your leadership team the status of the identified key threats and actions being taken to address them.

Who are your internal and external stakeholders and how will you partner with them?

Understanding the logic and limits of one's formal power is a key to success in a new role. Many new senior leaders are surprised to find that they have less formal power to make changes than they assumed. A variety of constraining forces restrict what can be done and how quickly. Leadership impact comes, in part, by leveraging existing relationships and building new coalitions. Each transition plan should have a section on stakeholder relations, as these partnerships are essential to a new leader's success.

Some leaders interpret stakeholder work as a political activity (and therefore somehow discreditable or unimportant) when, in fact, it is vital in exerting influence in a new role. We believe that the best leaders understand the importance of stakeholders, prioritize them, and then build partnerships with those who will make the greatest difference in regard to what the leader wants to achieve. Stakeholder building is not about accumulating personal power but, instead, getting things done through relationships with others. Formally or infor-

Seek the optimal margin of illusion.

mally, the most effective leaders develop a stakeholder map that includes targeted individuals and the actions that the new leader will take over the first year to promote these relationships.

One approach we recommend in some high-level transitions is to engage key stakeholders early in the new leader's tenure by asking them to answer a subset of the questions in the sidebar on page 47 (for example, What do you see as the new leader's key priorities in the first year?). The new leader or an external consultant can conduct this diagnostic. A summary is developed of the input from the stakeholder interviews and suggested recommendations for the new leader over the first six months. The transitioning leader then shares the feedback and draft plan with his or her supervisor, and in some cases the leadership team, to ensure alignment on the path forward. New leaders will also want to develop a communication plan that outlines types of communication that will be needed during the first year for key groups. For example, the leader may want to outline the firm's annual priorities in January and then review progress in town halls on a quarterly basis.

Gaining Necessary Support

- Who are the four or five key stakeholders (individuals or groups) with whom you need to build relationships? Why are they important?

- What actions will you take with each during your first six months to build partnerships with these individuals and groups? How will you assess your progress over time?

- What are the elements of your communication plan? Which groups (internal and external) need to hear from you and on which topics? On what topics do you need to hear from them?

Maximizing Transitional Success

Transitions require that a leader be supremely confident in meeting the challenges of a new role—but at the same time recognize that a past history of success doesn't ensure future success. Stated differently, leadership confidence is an absolute necessity in addressing a set of transitional challenges for which one is never fully prepared. In fact, those who believe they are better than they are are often more likely to act decisively and withstand the setbacks they will inevitably experience in a new role. Some describe this as the optimal margin of illusion for a new leader.

On the other hand, confidence can easily evolve into arrogance, resulting in blindness to the realities of the new environment and the potential pitfalls facing a new leader. In these cases, a new leader can make fatal mistakes based on confidence in his or her belief in what is needed. This is particularly true of leaders who have a history of uninterrupted success in past roles. Transitions are important because they force leaders to be confident but not arrogant—and to question the utility of past ways of thinking and behaving as they face unique challenges in their new roles. The best leaders develop a broad range of perspectives and capabilities as they progress through each career transition—with the most important being the ability to deal with the increasing complexity and uncertainty of senior-level roles.

Robert Bruce Shaw is an organizational consultant located in Princeton, New Jersey. He works with senior leaders and their teams on strategy deployment, organizational design, and leadership development. He has authored a number of books and articles on organizational performance, including "Trust in the Balance: Building Successful Organizations on Results, Integrity and Concern," "Discontinuous Change: Leading Organizational Transformation," and "Organizational Architecture: Designs for Changing Organizations." His most recent articles are "Organizational Bystanders" and "Building Better Leadership Teams."

Michael M. Chayes is managing principal of Sustained Leadership LLC, with a focus on coaching senior leaders for increased personal effectiveness, and consulting on executive and senior team alignment, leadership development, and organizational innovation and performance improvement. In past roles, he was lead partner at PricewaterhouseCoopers LLP, where he created and led the Organization and Change Strategy practice, and a senior director at the Delta Consulting Group, providing executive consultation to CEOs and their teams.

RESPONDING TO NAYSAYERS AND SKEPTICS

Like so many of us, you have probably been there before, in a meeting room, standing in front of your colleagues, PowerPointing your way to getting buy-in on a business plan. You're just about to start the wrap-up when the saboteur strikes: "But we tried that two years ago and it didn't get us anywhere. And you think it's going to work now, in this economy?"

At best, the saboteur is a skeptic, but at worst—as is usually the case—you're facing a *naysayer,* someone who makes a habit of shooting people down, whether in a business meeting or at the local pub. "The role of a naysayer is a natural one," says Lorne Whitehead. "He or she is out there in all parts of society. It's simple human nature."

Whitehead is the-coauthor of *Buy-In: Saving Your Good Idea from Getting Shot Down.* Along with Harvard Business School professor John Kotter, Whitehead has written a virtual one-stop reference resource for turning congenital saboteurs or mere critics into true believers.

Whitehead and Kotter's advice for neutralizing critics and getting buy-in is counterintuitive. "It is much more effective to engage your attackers and draw them in than to draw a line and confront them," says Whitehead, who is Leader of Education Innovation at the University of British Columbia. "People, and I mean naysayers, will respect you more if you respect them, namely by acknowledging them and their criticism.

Don't push the troublemakers out; let them in.

Also, their attacks draw attention to your proposal and attention is very valuable. And, if you handle the attack well, you'll look good and win credibility.

The coauthors describe five tactics for disarming critics:

- Don't push the troublemakers out; let them in and allow them to shoot at you. Letting people in gets their attention, and when people pay attention their minds are engaged and you can get the intellectual and emotional commitment you need.

- Don't respond by giving a speech or dumping loads of data. Keep your response short so that minds don't have time to wander. Use common sense, not lists or data, and speak clearly, using simple, direct language.

- Don't get personal, no matter how badly you want to. "Disrespect is negative," says Whitehead, "and even though some attackers are narcissists or bullies, if you respect them you will draw an audience emotionally to your side."

- Keep your eyes on the whole group and don't get hung up on the attacker. You're not trying to win over those who want to shoot down a good idea; you're pursuing the majority of those that determine whether you will win or lose.

- Don't try to wing it. Prepare well and try to anticipate attacks. If the stakes are high you may benefit from holding a small brainstorming session to review and prepare for the different types of attacks you think are possible. And don't ever become defensive.

In their book, Kotter and Whitehead list 24 attacks that are the most common and offer the response to each that is likeliest to defang an attacker. They group the set into three broad categories:

Category One: "We don't need your idea, because the 'problem' it 'solves' doesn't exist."

Attack Example: "We've never done this in the past, and things have always worked out okay."

Response: "That's true. But surely we have all seen that those who fail to adapt eventually become extinct." The response is simple, accurate, and basic. It essentially says that life evolves and to continue to succeed we must adapt. Examples will help your case.

Category Two: "Okay, there is a problem but your idea is not the solution."

Attack Example: "You're abandoning our traditional core values."

Response: "This plan is essential to uphold our traditional values." An effective response is based on a simple insight. Much more often than not, a really good idea upholds key values in the face of change. For example, "Yes, we propose advertising for the first time. This is a good idea because it's needed to help us grow, which is essential to offering more jobs and promotion opportunities, which is what our founders really cared about. We're not abandoning our traditional values, we're upholding them."

Category Three. "Okay, there is a problem, and this is a good proposal to deal with the issue, but you'll never make it work here. It's too difficult to understand."

Attack Example: "Too many of our people will never understand the idea and inevitably they will not help us make it happen."

Response: "That's not a problem. We will make the required effort to convince them. It's worth the effort to do so."

"Whatever you do," cautions Whitehead, "don't be defensive. Always, always engage."

SUSTAINABLE APPROACHES TO HUMAN RESOURCES IN A VOLATILE WORLD

Human resources practices, long the platform on which many companies built competitive advantage,

may soon fail many of those same companies unless they start rebuilding those practices. This warning—and what companies must focus on to attract and retain the best talent—is contained in a comprehensive report on global HR published by the Boston Consulting Group.

"Whether it's because leaders have taken their eye off HR to manage the latest crisis or because companies have developed ad hoc programs at the expense of sustainable programs, the fact is that talent management has been neglected these last two years," says BCG's Steve Richardson. "Executives participating in our survey believe that managing talent, leadership development, employee engagement and strategic workforce planning are the critical HR capabilities going forward. Yet those same executives admit that their current practices for meeting these capabilities are inadequate."

The BCG report, *Creating People Advantage 2010: How Companies Can Adapt Their HR Practices for Volatile Times,* is based on the views of 5561 HR and business unit executives in 109 countries. "Those companies that understand that they must have sustainable approaches to their workforce—rather than allowing themselves to be buffeted around by reality—are the companies that higher talent is going to want to go to over the next 20 years," says Richardson. "These are the companies that are looking ahead. They're identifying the capabilities that they'll need and developing a systematic approach to building those capabilities."

Anticipating future capabilities is just one of the best practices that separate HR leaders from the laggards. "Leaders of top performers are more willing and able to use HR as a strategic partner," says Richardson. "The best-practice companies focus on being flexible, not on cutting back, and select and concentrate on fewer, carefully chosen initiatives than lower performers, who seem compelled to develop a program for every event or situation."

High performers also:

- Develop metrics to assess training programs, and measure their ROI.

Best-practice companies focus on being flexible, not on cutting back.

- Transform HR into a strategic partner of senior management and brand themselves as great companies to work for.

- Are very sensitive to the needs of newer workforce demographic segments, such as Millennials, who want to be engaged and close to decision makers.

- Recruit 50 percent of their top executives internally (while laggards recruit only 13 percent from inside).

- Are able to demonstrate that strong employee performance and rewards correlate to excellent financial performance.

Survey participants identified four practices that they say will be critical for holding on to top talent over the next 20 years: managing talent, improving leadership development, enhancing employee engagement, and strategic workforce planning. Yet at the same time, participants agreed that their firms' current practices are inadequate. Richardson assesses each of the four as follows.

Managing talent: According to one survey respondent, "The key differentiating element in banking is people. Products are imitated and technology can be bought. But people make the difference." And banking is not unique in this regard. Managing talent, which includes issues such as talent pools and effective staffing of leadership positions, is the most critical of the four issues

for executives. Yet BCG found that the overall corporate capability for managing talent is "only slightly better than it was in 2008," when BCG conducted a similar study.

Leadership development: Companies are too short-term oriented and not paying enough attention to a looming leadership skills shortage at senior levels, one that will peak between 2020 and 2030, in all industries and regions. "Leaders who have been spending less time on coaching and development these past two years need to reboot themselves and get back to training leaders so that these newer leaders will be ready to go out there when the economy improves," Richardson says.

Employee engagement: Cost cutting has demoralized employees, but leaders must enhance engagement— "the glue that binds employees together in common purpose," according to one survey participant—if talent is to remain with their current company. "For example, middle managers communicate company values and are responsible for the day-to-day running of the business. Yet they've been de-layered over the past two years, and have been disengaging faster than any other function. But they're crucial to turning their companies around."

Strategic workforce planning: "The time horizon for workforce planning should be at least as long as the one for strategic planning—five years or more," says Richardson, but only 15 percent of respondents said their companies deploy simple workforce supply models that project the number and types of jobs that will be needed—and only about two-thirds of those have models that are aligned with the business plan. And while some companies—most of them laggards—continue to cut payrolls, streamlined processes and flattened hierarchies enable a company to be flexible and avoid cutting staff.

Says Richardson, "Companies should see the gaps in their HR policies as a call to action that, properly addressed, will make them an employer of choice for the next 20–30 years."

FOR MORE INFO...

Additional readings and resources on the topics referred to in this issue.

Bright Future

Frances Hesselbein

My Life in Leadership: The Journey and Lessons Learned Along the Way (Jossey-Bass, 2011; 240 pages; $27.95)

What Leaders Need to Know About Human Evolution and Decision Making

Paul R. Lawrence

Driven to Lead: Good, Bad, and Misguided Leadership (Jossey-Bass, 2010; 336 pages; $40.00)

Why Some Leaders Succeed and Others Fail

Paul B. Thornton

Leadership: Best Advice I Ever Got (Wingspan, 2006; 136 pages; $15.95)

Leadership Begins with an Inner Journey

James M. Kouzes and Barry Z. Posner

The Truth About Leadership: The No-Fads, Heart-of-the-Matter Facts You Need to Know (Jossey-Bass, 2010; 224 pages; $24.95)

First, Lead Yourself

Richard L. Daft

The Executive and the Elephant: A Leader's Guide for Building Inner Excellence (Jossey-Bass, 2010; 336 pages; $27.95)

Managing Up the Generational Ladder

Larry and Meagan Johnson

Generations, Inc.: From Boomers to Linksters—Managing the Friction Between Generations at Work (AMACOM, 2010; 272 pages; $16.95)

Building High-Trust Organizations

Pamela Shockley-Zalabak, Sherwyn Morreale, and Michael Z. Hackman

Building the High-Trust Organization: Strategies for Supporting Five Key Dimensions of Trust (Jossey-Bass, 2010; 272 pages; $50.00)

Responding to Naysayers and Skeptics

John Kotter and Lorne Whitehead

Buy-In: Saving Your Good Idea from Getting Shot Down (Harvard Business Press, 2010; 208 pages; $22.00)

COMING IN FUTURE ISSUES

William C. Taylor
Are You "Humbitious" Enough to Lead?

Jack Trout
Why Do Bad Things Happen to Smart Leaders?

Daniel Burrus with John David Mann
Skip Your Biggest Problem

John A. Quelch and Katherine E. Jocz
Respect Your Customers

Gail T. Fairhurst
Leadership and the Power of Framing

Jill J. Morin
Defining and Expressing Organizational Authenticity

Thomas Kayser
Six Ingredients for Collaborative Partnerships

Howard Morgan and Joelle Jay
Preparing for the Talent Exodus Ahead

Patti Lee-Hoffmann
Discover the Secrets of Becoming a Great Place to Work

ABOUT THE LEADER TO LEADER INSTITUTE

Established in 1990 as the Peter F. Drucker Foundation for Nonprofit Management, the Leader to Leader Institute furthers its mission—to strengthen the leadership of the social sector—by providing social sector leaders with essential leadership wisdom, inspiration and resources to lead for innovation and to build vibrant social sector organizations. It is this essential social sector, in collaboration with its partners in the private and public sectors, that changes lives and builds a society of healthy children, strong families, decent housing, good schools, work that dignifies, all embraced by the diverse, inclusive, cohesive community that cares about all of its people.

The Leader to Leader Institute fulfills this mission by perpetuating and sharing Peter Drucker's legacy through a multi-media knowledge approach and a blended learning model that combines face-to-face and online learning including:

- **Online Global Resources** including leadership dialogues, global webinar series and distribution of electronic publications
- **Partnership and Collaboration Opportunities** across the sectors that provide new and significant experiences for learning and growth
- **Self-assessment Workshops** and strategic planning resources
- **Unique High-level Summits and Conferences** for leaders from all three sectors

With the goal of leading social sector organizations toward excellence in performance, the Institute has brought together more than 400 thought leaders to publish over twenty-seven books available in twenty-eight languages and the award winning quarterly journal Leader to Leader.

In 2006 the dramatic reality of a looming leadership deficit was revealed in the Bridgespan Group report, The Nonprofit Sector's Leadership Deficit, which described the need for more than 80,000 new social sector leaders per year by 2016. In 2009, Bridgespan's updated report, Finding Leaders for America's Nonprofits, indicated an expanding need at an accelerating rate. The deficit is moving to a crisis.

Building on our legacy of innovation, the Leader to Leader Institute explores new approaches to strengthen the leadership of the social sector. With sources of talent and inspiration that range from the local community development corporation to the U.S. Army to the corporate boardroom, we help social sector organizations identify new leaders and new ways of operating that embrace change and abandon the practices of yesterday that no longer achieve results today.

Get to Know the Leader to Leader Institute

See www.leadertoleader.org for information on our programs,
resources, and articles from *Leader to Leader*.
Become a member and support our work.

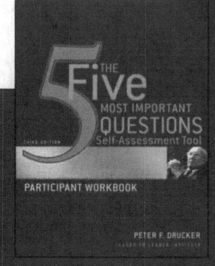

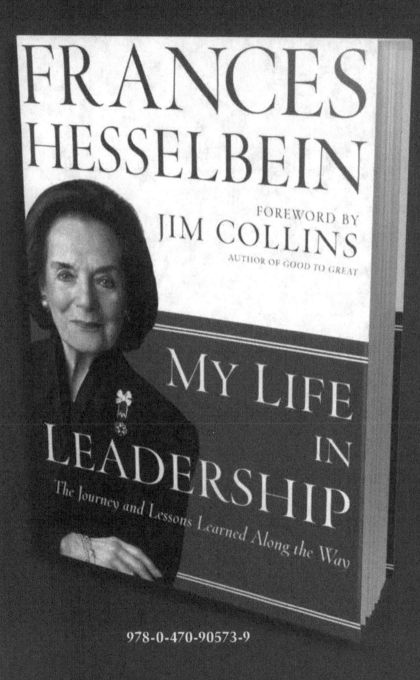